MEN SEEN

MEN SEEN

Twenty-Four Modern Authors

BY

PAUL ROSENFELD, *1890 - 1946*

Essay Index Reprint Series

BOOKS FOR LIBRARIES PRESS, INC.
FREEPORT, NEW YORK

First Published 1925
Reprinted 1967

PN
771
.R6
1967

LIBRARY OF CONGRESS CATALOG CARD NUMBER:
67-26776

PRINTED IN THE UNITED STATES OF AMERICA

To
SHERWOOD ANDERSON.

NOTICE

Unlike *Port of New York,* its predecessor, *Men Seen* is a miscellany. Its twenty-five chapters strive to paint no single picture, and the author is pleased that they do not. It has occurred to him that we contain two spirits, the one rejoicing in relieving the unity in things, the other rejoicing as positively in their multiplicity, their divergencies, and the exclusivity of their directions, and that we struggle to gratify them both. While getting *Port of New York* ready for publication last fall, the author was contented in working on the picture of a number of individualities moving through several gateways toward a common point. Vistas of a number of separate objects in motion through several gateways toward a focal point refresh him no less this year. And still, while kneading *Men Seen* into shape, he has found himself equally contented by a vista of an apparently very different sort, and gladdened that a number of men and women, related to each other in point of time and in medium of expression, remain a number of distinct objects moving out through their own doorways in directions entirely their own. And he has found himself richly indifferent to the fact that certain of his chapters stand reconstructions of material published several years ago; that not all of his volume greets the light of heaven for the first time; and that he has to express indebtedness to the editors of *The Bookman, The Dial, The Freeman, Manuscripts, The New Republic,* and *Vanity Fair,* for permission to reprint matter which has appeared upon their pages. It appears miscellaneousness itself is perfectly capable of being felt as an idea. Nor can it be so uncommon, the happy realization that the world is filled with individual, separate destinies, with more than a single career which has to be lived, and that all beings have their own unpredictable, independent miles to traverse. Many men must have it at some moments. Yet it is heartily to be desired it should be even less uncommon, particularly in the United States. The sense so beautifully breaks the monotonousness of the scenery alongside people's routes. It spares poor men the misery of having to tread their own strait pathways without end. Is not another of its names Imagination, and another still, Democracy? There can be nothing surprising then in the circumstance of a scribbler happy in having it represented by a book.

P. R.

February 14, 1925.

CONTENTS

x   *Contents*

MEN SEEN

GABRIELE D'ANNUNZIO

THEY knew so positively, the newspaper editors and their letter-writing subscribers, why the tragi-comic misdeed of Fiume had occurred. The *coup* had scarcely been struck before one heard on every side solemn tones affirming that energy had been perverted and our dilapidated dwelling-place made to crumble further because a poet had entered the "world of affairs." Gabriele d'Annunzio was the anomaly "the poet in the world of action." Yet, might it not have proven wiser of them, the editors and the suddenly-illuminated readers, had they hesitated modestly awhile before attributing the imbroglio of the Adriatic to the fact that a poet had overstepped the boundaries of the sphere assigned him by nature, and refrained from warning the tribe out of the province of serious affairs? It appears that in past

times certain artists showed themselves
not to completest disadvantage in the very
sphere of business, politics and warfare
termed by the American business man "the
world of action." It even seems that some of
them performed mildly respectable deeds in
it. Michelangelo, for example, does not stand
entirely besmirched for having ceased work on
the Medici tombs in order to fortify Florence
against brutal Emperor and treacherous
Pope. Milton is not blamed for having accepted the post of Latin Secretary to the
Commonwealth, and sacrificed eyesight and
fortune in behalf of civil and religious freedom; nor is Byron, for dying at Missolonghi
that Europe might be saved from the reac-
tionary schemes of the Holy Alliance. These
instances, and several commonplace others,
ought they not have deterred d'Annunzio's
critics a little from attributing the folly of his
course entirely to the limitations of the artistic
temperament? To us, it appears they ought;
and that sincerity, a modicum of general in-
formation, and a slightly diminished eager-
ness to discredit the image of the artist, would
have sent them probing for roots in the hero's
orchid-like personality. His poetical crea-

tions were at hand; and d'Annunzio's works
are extremely competent to show to disinterested minds that the psychic curve of
Fiume was plotted long before the garish day,
and that the riddle proposed by d'Annunzio
the freebooter is easily to be solved from a
reading of the relationships existing at all
times between him and his literary media.

D'Annunzio in his prose and poetry is a
man exaltedly laboring to heave a leaden
weight from his limbs. He has borne witness in a thousand forms to an indwelling
death. "Would that I might cease being
merely the brain, and come to love the world!"
he makes Giorgio Aurispa, one of his mouth-
pieces, cry.

> "Or chi,
> Dimmi, domò col fuoco il fuoco? Or chi
> Spense la face con la face? Or chi
> Con l'arco ferì l'arco?"

he writes upon the title-page of *Fedra*.
"There is no other fashion of obtaining victory over man and circumstance," he utters in
Il Fuoco, "than by constantly feeling one's
own exaltation, and magnifying one's own
dream of beauty or of power." The figure of
the psychically impotent artist has always

haunted his imagination. In his earlier years, he wrote in succession the stories of the golden youth of modern Rome corrupted by the vicious great lady and rendered unable to accept the true love offered him; of the artist prevented from giving himself to anyone, and incapable of feeling anything but the devastating love of plastic beauty; of the noble maidens waiting dreamily among the rocks for the life that does not come to them, and the young man whose will "hangs unused at his side like a sword in its scabbard."

All his career he has searched avidly for sensation. Figured by the imagination of the general a sort of Dionysiac creature of poetic frenzies and searing lips, modern Sardanapalus of letters, artistic Vesuvius which inundates whole provinces with its outpourings and shakes Rome, Florence and Venice with the might of its travail, d'Annunzio has in truth been spending his days in the frenetic quest of a situation, a posture, a movement. He has given himself innumerable forms of expression not quite compatible with the life of art, played at times the dandy and the voluptuary, the aviator and the sportsman, the demagogue and the soldier. Never has he ceased being impelled to display himself to the world in bizarre and arresting attitudes; and d'Annunzio has always been one of the most astute of self-advertisers, as though secretly convinced that a certain consummation would come to pass could men but be compelled to marvel at him, and admire and applaud. His search for the doctor has never been discontinued. He has tested in turn the radically opposite ideas of many men, of Wagner, Nietzsche, Tolstoy, Barrés. Like the true hypochondriac, d'Annunzio has swallowed every new nostrum placed upon the market. Year after year he has constituted himself the prophet of a new god; and the new god has invariably contradicted the god of yesteryear. At first, it was the religion of art which he preached, the virtue of form, sound and color. Then, it was the cult of extraordinary personages, the quest of the Latin superman, the renaissance of the Mediterranean genius. Again, in brief succession, it was the worship of the Latin soil and the Latin dead; the glory of machinery; *la mort parfumée;* the beauty of war and the grandeur of the Italian empire. Yesterday, we are told, it was the "league of suppressed nations." To-day, it is "the best elements of bolshevism." To-morrow, it will be something radically opposite. And it is the search for the intellectual medicine that, more than plain pagan love of magnificence and luxury, has incessantly impelled him to seek to live in the manner of a prince of the Renaissance. The rare and costly objects with which he has ever surrounded himself, the treasures of art, the statuary, the gorgeous manuscripts, the packs of hounds and the Arabian steeds, the marble victory that extended the conqueror's bays from the foot of his sumptuous bed, have been so indispensable to him indubitably for the reason he has always remained desirous of discovering through their works a secret power possessed by the great creators.

His art is external, predominantly. We are not penetrated by his compositions. We are not implicated in his murders and adulteries, his incests, parricides and fratricides, as we are in those represented by the dramas of the Greeks and the Elizabethans. His violent and smoky actions remain strangely matters of convention; gestures of grand operatic libretti. It is entirely immaterial to us whether the son murders the father in *La*

Figlia di Jorio or the father the son; whether Marco Gratico stabs Gergio Gratico or Gergio, Marco, in *La Nave*. It does not matter to us, save as picturesque detail matters, that the sixth-century Venetians of the later tragedy intone a profane hymn with the refrain—

> Domuit Diona fortes,
> Fregit Diona vires,
> Omnes trahit Diona.

and indulge in other sinful heresies. We can not identify ourselves with any of his wordy heroes. Something kin to relief seizes us when Aurispa throws his mistress and himself over the precipice. Certainly, *Il Trionfo della morte* is one of the dullest of erotic legends. Throughout the body of d'Annunzio's thickly jewelled work, one is conscious of that "aridity of agitation in which the narrator expends treasures of art in trying to interest us" found characteristic of all the man's prose by Henry James. His compositions remain feats of a virtuosic genius, brilliant displays of transcendent style, *bravura* passages upon the instrument which the author has shaped for himself with infinite care. Let him operate from the creative centers of others; oppose him with the

rarest works of art and of technique; and his
style rises to meet the stimulus freighted with
new colors, new scents, new textures. The
heaviness of Venice is in *Il Fuoco* as in no
other book; the splendor of machinery in
For se che si, for se che no as in the rhapsody
of no *dada* Frenchman. Superficially, the
story of Duse is the most flamboyant book, as
Le Vergine is the most shadowy, umbrage-
ous. Had they to crown the author upon the
Capitoline, they might justly do it with the
title "giver of handsome spectacles." But
ideas he has scarce any, and they only the
ghosts of the ideas of others. He remains the
master of fireworks; style as fireworks that
meet the ear and the palate and the palm as
well as the eye. *Francesca da Rimini* is
merely a gorgeously draped melodrama, a museum of terrible and interesting thirteenth-
century Italian antiquities. The few lines in
the fifth canto of the *Inferno* remain in-
commensurably more powerful than this erudite five-act tragedy. *La Figlia di Jorio* and
Fedra are equally gorgeous reliquaries, the
one in the pastoral-tragic, the other in the
classical-erotic vein; mosaics of astonishing
rhetoric, fantasias of words collected from a

thousand obscure and forgotten sources; objects incrustated with all manner of verbal preciosity.

D'Annunzio has never felt. In all the affairs of life he has been what he was to his divine mistress; the man who could not give out from his breast. For this reason, then, his poetical activity has become a form of compensation: protest of a rich and energetic nature against an inward incapacity. It is about his proper person that his works have been built. It is toward himself his energies are directed. We see him laboring for the summit of emotion; contorting his muscles; pumping and panting and straining in a sort of terrible tumescence. We feel him whipping himself relentlessly into the state of frenzy which he terms "condition of energy." He calls august and resonant names into his ears; he terms himself "Il Donnatore," Lord of Life, Gabriel of the Annunciation of a Latin Renaissance, descendant of a great family, demoniac like Socrates, inheritor of the imperious will-power of the *quattrocento*. In writing *Le Martyre de Saint Sebastien* in obsolete verse-forms of old French, he tells himself that his new muse resembles Valentina

Visconti, the Milanese princess who married into the house of Valois and became the mother of Charles d'Orleans and the foster mother of Dunois. He imagines himself in glorious situations; for his heroes, Andrea Sperelli, Giorgio Aurispa, Stelio Effrana, are frankly auto-portraits; sees himself inflaming with marvelous language an assemblage of highborn Italians in the hall of the Great Council in the palace of the Doges, while upon him there rest the ecstatic eyes of Eleanora Duse; sees himself surrounded by brilliant and wonderful disciples who strangely resemble himself; promises that through himself his countrymen are to receive a body of art which will be able to stand strong and erect under the cloudless Mediterranean sky and in the heat and abundance of the South; pictures himself, in *La Gloria,* conquering and dominating the Third Rome.

His passionate personages, Francesca, Mila, Fedra, Basiliola, are not so much personages as states of incandescence into which d'Annunzio strives to project himself. He would embody these legendary figures of romance in himself in order to be drunken with their passion. When he makes Fedra utter her concerto of splendid language, her rhetorical description of her great love, when he makes her declare that the earth may bear countless days and countless men, untold corn and labor, wine and war and sorrow, but never again a love that is like unto the love of Fedra, it is himself that he is struggling to excite. So, likewise in all the frenzy of curses, the long ecstatic declarations of passion, the loud rhetoric of ideas, with which his work is incrustated. When he makes the Deaconess Ema hurl shrill and decorative curses upon Basiliola in *La Nave;* when he makes the suitors of *La Pisanella* damn each other in seven different meters, he does so in the vain effort to fire himself with the ardor of hate. The harmony of stars which Basiliola vaunts herself to be, from forehead to heel; the flood and the ebb that sweep through her breast; the murmur of waters that sounds in her; the melody of worlds that lives in her; are but the symbols for the condition to which d'Annunzio has ever aspired and which he attempts to achieve by naming. Wellnigh each of his works contains some scene, some episode, that represents to d'Annunzio the coming of the power to feel. Such are the scenes where Mila is

roasted alive, where Fedra is transfixed by
the shaft of the goddess, where Aurispa hurls
himself and his mistress over the cliff, where
Saint Sebastien meets martyrdom, where
Basiliola slays the captives in the subterranean
prison, where the conflagration sweeps over the
water and ends the *Sogno d'un tramonto
d'autunno*. And for the reason that the pain,
the suffering, the agony, represents to him a
longed-for and beneficent condition, he makes
his characters utter the perversely ecstatic
language that has gotten him the popular
accusations of "degeneracy," has the daughter
of Jorio scream *La fiamma e bella! La
fiamma e bella;* has Fedra, expiring, joyously
salute the stars shining above the portal of
death; lets the prisoners offer their bare
breasts to the murderous arrows of Basiliola
and die praising her; lets the saint call to the
archers who are discharging their shafts at
him

> Je vous le dis, je vous le dis:
>   Celui qui plus profondément
> me blesse, plus profondément m'aime.

Between the rape of Fiume and d'Annunzio's characteristic literary work there lies
only a difference of medium. The use to which

the man has put the instrument of political action is precisely that to which he has so often put the belletristic. The escapade, too, is an act of false heroism, a parade chiefly for the benefit of the immobile spectator in d'Annunzio's mind. It is d'Annunzio's later attempt to rouse that spectator, to intoxicate him, to make him act; and the fact that the deed has won d'Annunzio the applause of fashionable Italy does not make it any less the piece of auto-intoxication. To a degree, it is the man's supreme effort. It was for the sake of this effort, which he knew the war would permit him to make, that he had welcomed the war long before the day when Italy joined in the fray, long before the days of the black August, and never had let slip the opportunity of preaching the beauty of carnage, the splendor of the "energy" it liberated. For its sake he restlessly inflamed the herd-pride of his countrymen by informing them that they were the rightful heirs of the Roman and Venetian empires; never had ceased crying of the Adriatic *fiat mare nostrum,* and congratulating the nation on the exploits of its soldiers in the raid on Tripoli. For it had been the great voice of modern Italy, the Italian Wagner, that his creative impotence had made him dream of becoming. It was as the Gabriel of the annunciation of a Latin renaissance that he had wished to appear to his compatriots. He had even told them in *Il Fuoco* that he was going to give them an art which would "sum up within itself all the forces latent in the hereditary substance of the nation; be a constructive and determining power in the Third Rome, pointing out to the men who were taking part in its government the primitive truths that were to be made the bases of the new forms; create instantaneous beauty in the numberless obscurities of the soul; bring to rough, unconscious souls, by the mysterious power of rhythm, an emotion deep as that felt by the prisoner on the point of being freed from his chains." On the Janiculum, he had promised, there was to arise, "where once the eagles had descended with their prophecies, a theatre of Apollo that was to be no other than the monumental revelation of the idea toward which the Italian race is led by its genius."

Of course, no new Bayreuth had risen, no new *Ring des Niebelungen* had been composed. D'Annunzio's "ideas," so cleverly adopted from Wagner, from Nietzsche, from

Barrès, had not been received with enthusiasm even by the gilded youth of the kingdom. Despite *La Figlia di Jorio* with its pompous dedication to the soil and the dead of Italy; despite the ideal of "energy" which d'Annunzio had held out to the young men of his country in the character of Hippolytos in *Fedra;* despite *La Nave* with its glorification of Italian sea-power, his works had not imposed themselves as the "monumental revelation." Indeed, the only "idea" to which fashionable Italy had been at all responsive before the recent war was that of imperialism. So d'Annunzio must have found himself secretly assured that, could but Italy be forced into a war and the imperial mania be made general, the miracle for which he had always longed would certainly come to pass in him. He would find himself voicing the universal sentiment. And, scarcely had the conflict swept over Europe than d'Annunzio began making his last great assault upon himself. Since the black hour he let slip no opportunity of exhibiting himself, of intoxicating himself, of glorifying himself. He offered the world every spectacle which he has been able to devise. We saw him harangue the Romans from the Capitoline;

receive the roses of Bari in token of the war-
will of the Italian people; sup with the king in
the Quirinal; deliver orations to the corps of
aviators; hail the constellation in the banner of
the United States when America entered the
war; fly over starving Vienna when Austria
crumbled; sing the *Cantico per l'ottava della
vittoria*. We have seen him seize Fiume, the
sinister banner of Italian imperialism at the
masthead, and strike the tottering edifice of
civilization another blow; hurl grandiose defiance at the Roman cabinet; issue manifestoes,
pronunciamentos, declarations, ultimatums;
arrange Homeric funeral rites in the great
square of Fiume for two soldiers dead of the
chicken-pox; offer to fly to China; espouse the
cause of suppressed peoples; enroll himself de-
fender of "the best elements of Bolshevism";
stand before the cameras of the cinematograph
photographers and place a helmet on his head.

Still, the miracle has not taken place.
D'Annunzio has found himself neither an
Achilles nor a Homer; neither a Byron nor a
Wagner. All his mimicry of heroic gestures
has not made him the creator; made him
neither the hero nor the poet. That we know.
We know that his deed is only an empty flour-

ish, whatever its immediate consequences may be. We know it, because never before have we so clearly known in what the creative act consists, and what it is the world demands of the poet and the hero alike. The poet is the man who projects an image beyond himself. His deed is feeling: demonstration of some finer order latent in men; manifestation of the spirit which the institutions and powers of this world crush from the human breast. This is the affirmation the artist makes, in letters and in politics, in every medium; this is the demonstration Michelangelo made in the Medici chapel and in the fortification of Florence alike; and Milton in *Samson Agonistes* and in his secretarial activities, and Byron in *Don Juan* and at Missolonghi. And we to-day inhabit a world that above all other worlds requires such testimonials. But it is precisely a testimonial to the spiritual might of men that Fiume is not. It is but another triumph of the past in man, all the more complete because it is the work of one who more than any other of his time has mouthed words concerning the glory of art, the grandeur of the poet, the genius of the race.

Were there no prose and poetry to demon-

strate the profound spiritual impotence of
Gabriele d'Annunzio, this escapade of his
would amply do so. And over his head we
send our cry for the true poet, the man who
can give the race the direction in which it
has to go.

JAMES JOYCE

JAMES JOYCE

A PARASITE inhabits our poor skulls. The little pest arrived from somewhere out in the dark, and now he occupies the premises and does there what he will. He walks into the house, sits down uninvited at the table and gobbles our best food. Our best moments are no longer our own; Mr. Mind has to come between them and us; he has to come between us and everything living and eternal as though he were jealous. Only yesterday he tried to force the wife, and stores of energy and direction are wasted in his innumerable grotesqueries and irrelevancies. There is no detail too trivial to excite his interest; out it must come upon the carpet, the silly or disgusting thing, and be made the object of attention. In all kinds of weather he must be showing us old forgotten faces, poisonous memories, humiliating episodes, and setting ancient music-boxes playing their nostalgic tunes. And the muck which he insists carting in from the streets! For all his fever of quotation from the Bible, Shakespeare and Alexander Pope, his favorite reading appears to be the Police Gazette; and he keeps a collection of smutty postcards bought in Paris, too. Besides, the pretentiousness of the creature! You might suppose he had scientific training, always imitating the manner of research, forming pseudo-scientific conjectures, demonstrating connections where no connections exist, and overlooking perfectly obvious examples. And there is no arresting him once he begins his unholy acrobatics. He will patter and spring about all night up in his apartment, moving all the furniture and making rest impossible; and often daylight supplants darkness before he consents to get into bed like an honest man and go to sleep.

How long a time he has bedeviled us we cannot exactly estimate. It is quite recently only that we have begun growing conscious of his antics, and taken to keeping him a little under surveillance; indeed, it is *Ulysses* that has succeeded in awakening us. Men before James Joyce have been aware of the parasitic and independent nature of our upper-story lodger, yet the Irish poet can fairly pretend to being his artistic discoverer and portrayer

of his form. The protagonist of his vast novel
is no creature of flesh. The hero of the
Odyssey may have been an individual. But
the being whose wanderings are set forth in
the modern tragi-comic parallel is no other
than "mind in the making," perceived
through types of the floating dislocated intellect of our time. With Joyce, a new comedy
comes to stand beside the old divine and
human comedies, the *comédie intellectuelle.*
He has placed the interior soliloquy of the
human being on a plane and a parity with his
exterior "action," and boldly mixed the two.

He has represented mind's play, the manner
of drunken existence led by him, with a queer
gusto at once sour and Rabelaisian, with pity,
tenderness and Irish mischief, and upon an
heroic scale and with heroic richness of
illustration. And none of Joyce's coevals,
neither Miss Stein nor Miss Richardson nor
Ernest Hemingway, has made it an object of
contemplation with a relentlessness and brav-
ery in any way comparable to his. Quite as
the painted slides of glass in medical museums
give in finest segments the physical aspects
of the brain, so does his method render all the
stratas of mind in their manifold interpene-

trations. We are shown the mind we reveal
to each other; and the mind full of fears and
fantasies, monkey-like preoccupations and
ignoble interests which we try to reveal to no
one and to keep utterly to ourselves; and,
through representations of the dreamlike and
hallucinatory states in which the activities of
the brain assume a definite corporeality, the
mind which seeks to conceal itself and its fixa-
tions and traumas and outlawed impulses from
ourselves, too. We are shown its motion, its
rattling activity, broken rhythms, starts, attitudes and relationships, and made to observe
it under the influence of bodily states, colored
and given form and direction by emptiness of
stomach and repletion of stomach, alcoholic
intoxication, evacuatory functions, sexual
periodicity, fatigue, and play of light and tem-
perature and dark.

The minds of three almost heroically established, and of numerous minor characters, are
emptied of their contents before us; and each
of the expositions demonstrates amid individual variations the general character of the
lodger, and gives the rich comedy of mind's
extraordinary depth and extraordinary shal-
lowness and limitation. *Ulysses* begins with

the presentation of the interior of Stephen
Daedalus; and Stephen is at once a separate
organism moving through the Dublin of the
new century, and a very large slice of the
poetic aspect of the contemporary mentality.
The fellow is a genius, as certainly as only a
few characters in fiction are geniuses, Julien
Sorel, perhaps, and the Prince of Denmark.
He has the distinction and the nobility of
Hamlet, and like Hamlet, "wherever he is, he
is alone." But not even Hamlet is plunged
into as great a separation and remoteness
from what lies round him, as this figure in
shabby black and cast-off shoes. Stephen is
resourceless in the world. A current of restless melancholy thinking and broken music
enislands him, feeding upon him, playing with
itself, and removing his interest from the exterior world. He feels with an intensity and
purity unknown to the louts about him; where
they see commonplace figures, an old woman
who brings the milk, say, he perceives the ancient culture and beauty and courtesy of his
race. But what he feels in these instantaneous
flashes he cannot express. The bewildering
jumble of "voices," of memories and reflections of the old poets and philosophers, echoes

of a scholastic Catholic world long since dead, and magnificences of churchly litanies and languages no longer spoken, resume their current. Trivial and disgusting details obtrude; compulsive impulses arise and insist on ridiculous obediences; alarms and apprehensions shake and weaken him without cessation. A terrible and defensive pride treasures the wounds given it by people, by life, and broods on the guiltiness of deeds done upon him. Visions of outcasts and disinherited men and men betrayed by Ireland come to wring his heart; bony hands are forever laying themselves on his arm bidding him be faithful and remember. But he himself is pursued by furies and lashed by conscience, whence the blamefulness and judgment. He suffers from an "agenbite of inwit," remorse for a sin of which his reason has absolved him but of which he cannot wash himself free; and finally his mind invests an hallucination with all the human piteousness he had found in his own mother, and all the reverence wakened in him by the church, and strikes his spirit down.

It is the content of the mind of Mr. Leopold Bloom, unrolled by the incident of a day of peregrination and adventure, and exposed like a film, which constitutes the major portion of the Gargantuan book; and the mind of the wandering, absurd and kindly Dublin Jew reveals upon its different foundation, and through a different texture, an indirection, intrustiveness and dislocation similar to that of Stephen's. The youth's fine mind is suffused by the tradition of a perished poetry and scholasticism, and blows like a fallen leaf from out the medieval world. But Bloom's is almost empty of positive tradition. It is the amazing flower of what Houston Stewart Chamberlain has called the Chaos of the Peoples. Mr. Bloom is sympathetic, helpful, liberal, free of the vulgar prejudices and patriotic paranoias of his fellow Dubliners, and filled with the "culture" broadcast by popular education. He seems to have been bred upon newspapers and newspaper talk. If his mind is alert, curious, interested, it is overcrowded by pseudo-scientific postulations, modern superstitions, useless and bawdy perceptions and ridiculous relations. He does not think as Stephen does, in images; his mind is concrete and sentimental; yet it too stands between its host and existence, half jester and half tyrant. Bloom never quite synchronizes

with the rhythm of what exists without him;
he is superior to it and yet perpetually vic-
timized by it. It is obvious that his mental
activity is an evasive mechanism. There is a
painful knowledge with which he is perpetually
playing hide and seek, and which he seeks to
evade through an interest in exterior objects.
Joyce has very playfully placed this mind
under the sign of the modern scientific spirit.
In the phantasmagoria of hallucination in the
Nighttown chapter, a very developed masochistic tendency reveals its existence, and
shows the wilfulness of the facts disordering
and disequilibrating the mind.

Last, outspreading like a wide pool, slow
finale of the great movement as Daedalus' intellect is its initiator, the contents of the mind
of Marion, sumptuous, delightful, unforget-
table partner of Mr. Bloom; and a third important aspect of the mentality of an autoerotic
age is manifest. Marion is warm, voluptuous,
and fond of giving pleasure; she is a kind of
artist strewing seeds with liberal hand; and
men procure an extraordinary release from
her. Yet it appears she too like her spouse and
young Stephen is cerebral and a solitary. But
a few hours' since the burning Blazes Boylan

has departed her promiscuous couch, her thoughts form a slow warm current in which she lies as in a bath. Mind interferes here, also, one would say. She does not appear ever to have gotten entire satisfaction. Some dainty and imaginative vein in her has never been expressed; she lies a prey to an intellect using her body for its own morose delectation; and her genuine satisfaction comes, we perceive, not from doing, but from thinking about that which she has done.

A marvelous hand has given form to these vagrant minds. Through a sensuous material, Joyce has fixed the quality of flow in progress within Stephen, Bloom, Marion, and such subsidiary characters as the irate citizen, Gerty MacDowell, the pursy priest, the drunken soldier and the others. It exists for us in the shape of a hard, gamey and refreshingly comical prose. An exquisite refinement of the ear seems to have constituted the apparatus; it is not difficult to connect the James Joyce who dreamt of cultivating his voice for concert use with the author of the marvelous word-structures of *Ulysses*. These are patently the expression of a sovereign sensitivity to the music of words, and delight in their

brute forms and combinations. Joyce seems
to hear, through the imitations of the exterior
world and the ejaculations of an interior one
contained in language, the reports of the
senses, the indications of touch or sight or
smell, and to taste them with the tongue, and
to express this content through verbal inter-
relations. No living author brings a vocabulary either as crisply, sharply, pungently used,
or as vasty. Joyce possesses a relatively unlimited knowledge of the resources of the English language. *Ulysses* is a reliquary of
sinewy terms. Words have been assimilated
from the writings of the Jacobeans and the
speech of the living, from all classes, profes-
sional men, bar-rooms, brothels, illiterates of
the slums, peasants, journalists, children.
Like Strawinsky, Joyce appears to prefer
turning to the city streets for his idiom, and
using it with all the fine crudity of a first-
year high-school boy. And the composition of
his savory vocabulary reveals an instinct for
rhythm equally developed. It is apparent
that Joyce has always heard more clearly the
way in which people speak than what it is they
have to say. His large work, like Shakespeare's isle, is "full of voices," many tones

and modes of expression, guttural inarticula-
cies, mellifluous rhetoric, hysterical soarings.
And it is filled with delicious parodies of many
inflated manners: Carlylese, American advertising, servant-girl romantic, pseudo-legen-
dary, jack-tar, polite and provincial jour-
nalese. A fragment recently published contrasts the tones of four Irishmen, one from
Ulster, one from Leinster, one from Munster
and one from Connaught. One remembers
with illumination the scene in the *Portrait of
the Artist as a Young Man* in which Stephen
becomes fully aware of his vocation, and real-
izes that he draws "less pleasure from the reflection of the glowing sensible world through
the prism of a language manycolored and
richly storied than from the contemplation of
an inner world of individual emotions mirrored in a lucid supple periodic prose."

Endowed in the shape of a feeling for words
and rhythms with a medium directly expressive of the most secret activities of the
human mind, Joyce is to be credited with having driven it uncompromisingly. His prose is
built relentlessly upon rhythm. For the sake
of presenting veraciously the manner in which
sensations skim into the brain, he opposes

words in heathen order, and reiterates them in varied combinations; for example—"Smack. She let free in sudden rebound her nipped elastic garter smackwarm against her smack-able, a woman's warmhosed thigh." Aggluti-nations in the Greek and German manners dot the prose—*scrotumtightening, woodshadows, bullockbefriending, mellonsmelloneous.* Con-crete images are invariably permitted to stand for the analyses of the reflective faculty— "Onions of his breath came across the counter out of his ruined mouth." Characteristically, all richness, fulness, all abundance of any positive kind is absent from the texture of the language. Joyce has very rightly kept it light and acrid. Stephen speaks of Shakespeare's "lean unlovely English"; but it is Joyce's own far more than Shakespeare's that has no fat-ness and juiciness. A sharpness and steepness of the senses records itself, a kind of famished sensuality which never soaked up sun and amused itself in a cellar. There is magnificence in Daedalus' mind; his language is exalted and lyric; but it is morbid and darkly jeweled.

Toward the conclusion of Marion's revery, something like a sunrise begins to steal over the prose; the language takes on some of the

warm ripeness of the woman's body. But that
opulent page merely intensifies the acridity of
all that has gone before. It carries an affirmation which recalls in its enigmaticality the
last terrible passage of *Le Tentation,* where
in the rising sun the saint perceives the
face of Jesus Christ. Yet upon its level
Joyce's prose is almost perfect. So utterly
faithful to his intuitions has he been that
a marvelous vitality inhabits each of his
phrases. One gets sensations from them as
from chords of music and nuclei of color.
If in *A Portrait of the Artist as a Young Man*
Joyce made a late addition to the body of pre-
raphaelite prose, and produced a book beautiful for its lyricism and soft and glowing
colors, in the enormous sequel he has satisfied
the more modern desire for hardness, sharpness, wildness in the way that steel construction and Strawinsky do. Naturally, it is not
to be maintained that the book is sustained
throughout upon a single plane of vitality.
Certain scenes, particularly the scene in the
cave of the winds, sometimes known as the
newspaper office, seem relatively slack and of
an inferior interest to us. Yet in its totality
the surface of *Ulysses* stands the work of an

incomparable art; and we feel at liberty to dance upon it, it is so solid, as upon a stone.

And, co-extensive with the unrolled films of mind, like mountain summits above foothills, rises a memory of the *Odyssey*. It is the final stroke of definition, this evocation. Certainly, the objects which have caught the wandering mind, and from which it can disentangle itself no more than a fly from flypaper, the stuffy properties of a world of troglodytes hopelessly poisoned by centuries of religion, ignorance and servitude, excrement and alcohol, alone are competent to emphasize its quality and give it spatial existence. The twenty-four hours indicate twenty-four years. And the tenuous, pathetic and absurd relationships existing between its individual bearers, and affirmed by the novelist's symbolism of action, stand additionally demonstrative of its final inadequacy and insufficiency. It is the business of intelligence to relate, and a sort of feeble relationship does spring up between Stephen and Bloom and Marion. Stephen is incapable, alone, of freeing himself from a fixation upon his dead mother, since the complex is intensified by the maryolatry of the church and the masochistic tendency of his race. (Joyce in one place significantly mentions the polo match *All Ireland* against *The Rest of Ireland*.) The man is a sport from an ancient herd-stem lost between a world dead to him and a world which he has not the power alone to call into existence. Hence, he is condemned to assume a passive attitude toward the members of his own sex: he is in search of a "father," and collapses grotesquely his head among the stars before the loutish soldier who has a King. He does appear, after his beating, to find a father surrogate in Bloom. For Bloom is the Co-human. Out of all Dublin he is paternal, pitiful, altruistic; and complements Stephen's character. Both men are outside the life that flows about, superior to it; but Bloom is free of some of the bonds from which Stephen cannot escape. He is "the South" in contrast to damp and illnourished Dublin; the Orient as opposed to the unvoluptuous Puritanical North; and the Synagogue, religion of God the Father, in contrast to Catholicism and its cult of the Virgin Mother and her Son. He is adjusted to life better than Stephen is. He lives by his wits, supports a wife and has raised a daughter, and enjoys himself as he trots about Dublin solicit-

ing advertisements. And he has a need for
an intrasexual relationship kin to Stephen's.
He is alone and outrageously cuckolded by his
wife. His son, who might have connected him
with Irish life, and given him adequate opportunity for transferring paternal feelings, is
dead. Besides, with all his muddle-minded-
ness and half-education, he has enough keen-
ness to recognize in Stephen the possessor of
the developed fineness and culture which persists in rudimentary form inside himself. A
transference is achieved. Unfortunately it
does not take place before some element of
pride or will has been shattered in the younger
man. A sinister quiet reigns over him the latter part of the story; and we are never assured
that the relationship with Bloom comes to
consciousness in him. And although Bloom is
more conscious than Stephen of the existence
of the tie, his awareness is dreamlike and
weak. The intercourse remains desultory; the
two men sit in the kitchen of Bloom's troglo-
dyte two-story dwelling, drink cocoa and spend
a pleasant hour talking. Then the poet goes
out into the night; Bloom gets into bed with
Marion, wakens her and then drops off to
sleep. And Marion, revolving in the Septem-

ber of her summer around her own axis, re-
lives the past buried inside her, imagines an
affair between herself and the young man of
whom Bloom has told her, and struggles des-
perately back toward the moment when first
she gave herself to men; while beneath her the
quoits of "Cohn's old bed" jingle as if in iron-
ical anticipation of the next occupant.

Again, the series of imaginary questions
and answers which represents the hour in
Ithaca, indicates by its stiffness the inadequacy of scholastic dialectic. But the
juxtaposition to the *Odyssey,* the parallel-
ism of title, personages and situations,
reinforces all Joyce's other methods of definition. It establishes with one large inclusive
stroke the quality of the material, and relates
it to the remainder of the universe. It lets the
light of the Homeric waterworld stream
through upon the amazing modern complex,
relieving both the profundity of the picture
of Joyce and his time, and its tragic limitation
and inadequacy. The mind of the living age
has gained prodigiously in variety of interest
and complexity over the ancient dreamful
one. It represents enormously intricate relationships, subtleties of contact, curious abut-

ments. It is chuckfull of items of knowledge
entirely unknown to the simple Greeks.
The Christian centuries have left plane beyond
plane of horizon about it. The twenty-four
hours of serio-comic activity chucklingly presented by James Joyce produce a slow painful
explosion in our picture of the universe. Since
one secondary capital in one single day exhibits as vast, as incommensurable and as in-
eluctable a series of events, the inference of
what takes place in twenty-four cities in a
single day, not to speak of what takes place in
twenty-four cities in twenty-four days, dazzles
the mind with an instantaneous sense of in-
finitude more gigantic than any we have ever
had. Yet in all its comparative simplicity and
childishness and dreaminess, the mind whose
form the *Odyssey* was, stands serene and eminent. It was fresh, faithful and melodious;
made a wondrous harmony of its component
elements, and held life in relation with eternal
things. It was an aid to lustiest living. But
our mind is stale and weary in its youth, dissonant, jumbled and out of tune with the
eternities as with itself. We exist it seems in
a crisis of its carbuncular adolescence. Destined it seems one day to be a god and harmon-

ize a mighty universe, richly amusing in its antics, it stands utterly balked viciously autistic, sluggish, disorientated, unable either to return into the dark warm unconscious out of which it came or to coördinate its faculties in advance; and quite as great a handicap to human life as an advantage.

So thoroughly is *Ulysses* the definition that it can even be found to indicate its own position among literary achievements. In holding his material against the *Odyssey* for the purpose of characterizing it as content, Joyce has also registered a judgment upon it considered as a literary form. The juxtaposition has accented the golden sonority of the ancient epic, and the lighter, bitterer, thinner of the modern one: it has placed Joyce and his work upon a level distinctly beneath that on which the singer of the old sea-wanderer and his hexameters stand. In performing this judgment Joyce once again has affirmed the wisdom of the race. For the *Odyssey* is an expression of a life completely used, exercised to the fulness of its capacity for tragedy and for delight, and deprived by death of nothing of worth. And men have always bestowed the prize and will always bestow the prize, out of the needs of life, upon expressions of this free sort. We cannot be sincere and not crave fullest living. We want what life does not wish to give. And men have always set the expressions of lives balked of great satisfactory play and held from the limits of the human frame, upon the lower plane; even though these very frustrate lives, by some heroic effort, by humor or by satire, have nevertheless managed to set their defeats outside themselves, and indicated the illimitabilities denied to them. We accept conscience of frustration only for the purpose of rejecting it for the human race. Yet it is no petty achievement to have attained with a serio-comedy the level upon which Swift and Flaubert stand, and long will stand. That also, like the very upper, lies high above the smoke of earth.

D. H. LAWRENCE

D. H. LAWRENCE

L AWRENCE is the Minnesinger returned
in a modern day. He is the Frauenlob
of the age of the war and its differentiating,
self-divided women. Above him there looms
single, all-encompassing like the bestarred
firmament itself, as once before it loomed over
the poets of the chatelaines, the magical shore-
less world of woman. It is about him an un-
explored region of inexpressible wonder and
terror, new, perilous and infinitely seductive.

Like the discoverers of the feudal woman-
soul, the being of this son of the Nottingham-
shire coal-country seems to have been rounded
and extended and made almost intolerably
sensitive through the new-come consciousness
of the eternally opposed principle. Like theirs,
his entire man appears to have been made a
pointed flame by the unappeasable desire to
press more and more of this warm enveloping
cloudland to him, to penetrate further and further into its virgin realm. They had no vision
come to them that was not a seeing of woman;

45

and he has not had another subject, in ecstasy
or bitterness, since a youth. His first book
showed him pressing timidly into the mysterious unillumined space which lies between the
warring sexes. He has never ceased from
wandering ever more deeply into it. It seems
as though his last word must be what Tristan's
was, and like his must be but the thousandth
repetition of the very first—"Isolde!"

This is not Don Juan come to woman in order that the icicle in his own breast may be
melted and he be left at last able to touch. It
is a man given new, increased and more complex capacities for feeling. Lawrence seems
to us the man who has appeared simultaneously
with the individualizing, breeched, self-conscious women of the new century; and armed
with a sense capable of following and making
respond and satisfying the new complex, stubborn, recalcitrant female types. Something
akin to what happened to men through women
in the twelfth century seems commencing a
parallel course. It was the sudden evolution
of the great countesses and heiresses, the sudden appearance in barbarous crusading Europe
of grave, delicate, haughty ladies in the don-
jon keeps, that forced the creation of the

courtly poetry. Men had to become conscious of these new senses and desires and minds under penalty of impotence. The Minnesingers, the type of men who cov'l understand and meet and checkmate thes: delicate and scornful dames, and who could interpret them and their world to other men, were developed. The proposition of new riddles and the creation of new intelligences for reading them has, perhaps, never quite left off since then. But in recent times, and even before Nora slammed the front door behind her, a sudden new crescendo has begun in the old process. It is no longer upon the isolated peaks of society that the development, the individualization of women has taken place, but in the great lower strata. Economic conditions apparently have made women the rivals of men, and made them independent of the family; but beneath the economic revolution there is the curious development in the substance of the race itself, the pushing away of people from the tribal types like twigs away from the parent branch; the departure of men and women from a kind of general soul that made them closely alike for all the differences of sex, out toward more sharply individualized characteristics. And in the separation, the facility for the meeting of spirits has become reduced. The capacity for satisfactory choice has produced in quantity a woman at war with her own sex, and a man subject to woman, incapable of developing beyond a rudimentary state his own masculinity, and unweighted and unconvinced in himself.

The consciousness developed by the experience of life in Lawrence is part of the new weapon capable of snatching for these divergent types the inheritance which life threatens to withhold from them. Itself builds the bridge between the man and the recalcitrant woman; creates a contact between the two polarizing individuals. The new sense is not what the awareness of Shaw and George and other scratchers of the sexual is: a conception, developed by men in whom habits of analysis and of abstraction have produced the severance of the different mental faculties, for the purpose of influencing their wills and making possible the elementary operations of the mind. It is a sort of genius; a power of entering sympathetically into the object and coinciding with it. It is an intuition of what goes on within the woman in her endless cycles of revulsion from and reference to the man; a capacity for following her in her flights from her own sexuality, and of meeting her in her strange sudden fluttering returns to it. Lawrence has developed vision in his chest. Crop of the dumb earthy English life, he has begotten knowledge of the human being where it is not separate from the earth; knows the life that went on in the human being before mind quit its dark and slumberous house, and proceeds still behind the intellectual screen. And it is as though the female in the man himself had suddenly become useful to him in helping him feel the world of the woman. He, the man, has dared to feel the secret life of the woman where she is female most. He is like one come by night to an ancient rock-temple avoided centuries long. In the dread precinct of the old heathen gods, in the spot of forgotten blood-rites and human sacrifices, the lairs of what reptiles and beasts of prey he knows not, he dares to stand, and to lift high his torch toward the forbidding front of rock. The flickering light falls upward upon mysterious sculptured forms. Black rude pilasters hacked from the wall of stone, heavy squat arches brooding over low forbidding portals, commence slowly to heave from the gloomy mass.

At one place the shine finds its way into the solid rock itself. He begins to perceive, cupping itself, the low secret cavern over which the temple was built to stand ferocious guard. Where the gods descended and it was death for the profane to look, the fireshine flows in and lets him see.

With minimum of friction the data of a new vision have passed through Lawrence. He stands eminent among the artists of the day for the faithfulness with which he delivers unrationalized and unproven perceptions. Mad unsupported intuitions that come to him are set forth with a gesture of utter trust in the power that brought them. No living writer relies less on outer authority, and more entirely on inner; and some fumbling experience inside us is left to grope toward his ejaculations of the truth and test them out by its proper lights. Lawrence has communicated through words an ocean of sensations of a new sharpness, thickness, warmth, instantaniety. Not indeed since Swinburne spoke of

> snow-soft sudden rains at eve

and

> Half-faded fiery blossoms, pale with heat
> And full of bitter summer

have words hissed and scratched and bubbled
and rendered bodily sensations as those written
by Lawrence when he is most moved. All the
senses are aplay all the time in him, it seems;
aplay almost to the point of excess. He knows
as few have known the tender caress lain by
softness upon the skin; and as few have known
the hardness and rawness and painfulness of
edges, points and stony mass. He has done
much to help restore to English some of the
forcefulness of expression taken from it by the
Victorians and preraphaelites. The style that
glows with color like Pater's and Ruskin's and
Rossetti's, and can lend itself to fullest description of the magnificences of earth, Syrian
moon-nights and cathedral feelings and Alpine
fields of snow, is nevertheless rapid, pungent
and homely. It is replete with the idiom of
the industrial Midlands in which Lawrence
was born and wherein he grew. It is full of
names redolent of the English countryside,
names of birds and names of flowers, and stout
Saxon farm-words. His vocabulary is particularly strong in verbs; everything is perceived
in movement, in process of acting or being
acted upon. And it is a spoken English he
writes. He is almost too meticulous in preserv-

ing the spontaneous gush of the language. And still, his writing is nearly always lyrical. He has a gift for the inevitable phrase, the inevitable metaphor. Original images gush from him in exhaustless fountain. Particularly *The Rainbow* and *Women in Love* are full of a rich poetry, nervous, tense and abrupt. The very abstract states of being which Lawrence loves to describe have a sensible color and weight and form, stand real and solid in the world of fact. The repetition of a cadence, the insistent reiteration of an adjective, communicate a mood with simplest machinery. At times he is wellnigh impotent before the image in his mind. We hear him stammer. We see the hands vainly sawing in the attempt to describe the feeling. But even these moments have their effectiveness in communicating something of his own ecstatic subjugation to his states.

The ideas with which the sensations come intertangled, and along which they are lain by the artist's hand, carry like them to the surface the unrationalized theater of life. Lawrence expresses numberless states of being that have lain hitherto underneath the lintel of the mind, and come strange to the day-pour like

islands cast up by submarine eruptions. He
gives the state of being in woman at the time
man comes to her without her wish; and the
state of the man after he has been thrust away
and the partner reaches again for him like
moonfire seeking the frozen ground; and the
state of sudden entrance into communion when
the taking of food becomes a sacrament, and
the earth is invested with prodigally scattered
jewels. He gives the fear men have for each
other in their resistance to the utter domination
of women; and the strange solidarity of
women, understanding each other without word
or gesture and leaguing together by strange
imperceptible subconscious signs; and the dark
resentment of women against the choiceless
man; and the blackness and recalcitrancy of
the man forced against his wish by the aggressive woman. He gives the feeling of dirtiness
and violation in the man submitted to the deliberate depression and emasculation of the
army-idea and the army-men; and the abstract
terror known to the individuals who during
the war could not be-muddy the god inside them
and give themselves prostitute-like to the spirit
of the obscene swarm. The feeling of closeness, tightness, overinhabitation of the British

island, every inch of ground known and lived
in and wakeful in the dark like a sleepless being is in his stories; the decomposition of the
European world-feeling on the American
prairies or mid the Australian bush, in criticism and fiction both. Out of him come figures
expressive of the state of man in this moment
of sexual upheaval: men able to love only their
own concepts and oriented to a static, mechan-
ized universe; boyish men sitting and watching
women a few years their seniors move about in
khaki breeches; smallish male tortoises following the lumbering female about the Italian
garden paths and biting at her heels; women
presenting each other with boldly colored pairs
of stockings; miners turning about and jeering
impotently at two women flaunting blue and
green-colored hose beneath short skirts. A
wizened passionless woman has to throw herself between a mating couple, and dies crushed
under the tree felled by the ax of the man. A
suffering soldier in a war-hospital begs a
woman to sew with her own inexperienced
hands some shirts for him and embroider them
with an old heraldic family crest. A man
stands by a southern ocean in the witch-magic
of a moon-night in spring, and feels deep

aloneness, and yearns for relationship limitless as the element before him.

Images of this character constitute the motives of nearly all the prose and the poetry of Lawrence, the travel-books, novels and fantasias alike. The years have merely produced modification in the form of them. The books, as Seligmann so clearly demonstrated in his study, reveal the stages by which, from its beginnings in subjection to the soul of woman, his own personality has groped through the war-crumbled world toward possession of itself in the shape of conviction, resoluteness and weight. For Lawrence is of the company of the men who breathe through art. Writing for him is the resolution of the universal internal conflict through dramatic representation. *Sons and Lovers* in the picture of lads left passive and choiceless through the familiar home-constellation of inferior, sensual father and superior, unsatisfied and resistant mother, expresses, for us, the root-form of the modern sexual tragedy. *The Rainbow,* Lawrence's great successful venture in abstraction, gives the woman putting sun and stars in her own hair, enveloping the man completely in the womb of her love, and yet unable to give herself completely to him.   The poem cycle *Look, We have come through,* gives the experience of partner-choice, man and woman working out a union through blood and pain.   *Women in Love* contains the tragedy of the man who cannot find any hold on life save through the woman; and *Aaron's Rod* shows men in the hideously vulgarized decayed world of after-war struggling for the independent hold subconsciously desired by the woman and compulsive of child-bearing.   And *Kangaroo* and *Studies in Classical American Literature* express the most recent stages of the battle.   Both deal principally with the relations of men to men, for the reason that the confusion in the relations between the two sexes has its counterpart in the confusion inside the bounds of the single sexes; and clarity of one relation cannot be gained without clarity of the other.   If the modern disintegration has expressed itself in the form of an irresolute male and an aggressive female, in the field of intrasexual relations it has expressed itself in American democracy, brotherly "love" flowing inevitably into war and destruction, and incapacity for creative coöperation. Manhood is a mystery, a self-sufficiency kin to the self-sufficiency of ocean and sky. It is aristocratic, for it believes in itself completely, and is capable of losing itself in an idea. And the men who open themselves up readily in sticky love for each other and envy every differentness, superiority, self-sufficiency of their neighbor; the men who have always to move in herds and remain nevertheless incapable of subordinating themselves for any purpose save destruction, and to any lord of life, stand in conspiracy against their own sex. It was natural that the vision of this division in psyche of the simple male of today should have come to Lawrence in reference to the Australian and American scene, the two most "democratic" of the English speaking countries; and that the assertion of an aristocratic faith should have been made in a volume of essays on classical American writers. For America began by slaying its father and with him every natural superiority and self-sufficiency. Its classical literature expresses the soul of man under the father-complex and therefore at war with the malest characteristics in itself. And America must either learn to subordinate itself to an idea, a religious feeling, a sense of the whole of life, or drag the white race down with it into slime.

What we have in Lawrence, then, is a writer of the company of the *grands écrivains*. It is an original mind giving itself in an easily original idiom; a nature pouring itself forth in "profuse strains of unpremeditated art"; a talent which, like that of the born race-horse, runs entirely for the love of the running. True, Lawrence at the age of thirty-seven odd years is still somewhat more the commencement of a great writer than the great writer fully fledged. He is not always successful in the organization of his material. Both his prose and his poetry have an immense claim on us for the reason that they always say something. But many pieces of his, novels, poems and essays, are not entirely accomplished forms existing with a life their very own. It is to be suspected that he is one of those introverted persons who find it difficult to view themselves objectively; and find almost insuperable obstacles barring their way to that point in which they are both the actors and the spectators of their own work, and capable of viewing it and criticizing it from the outside. For this reason, Lawrence the novelist

in certain of his novels is not entirely successful in defining his characters. He is too much
within them, feeling the world as they feel
it, and too little outside and above them, to
entirely define and individualize them. They
are real, but not sufficiently distinguished.

Hence the comparatively early *Sons and
Lovers* remains one of the most completely successful of Lawrence's novel-forms. The autobiographic nature of the material treated
therein relieved the author of the necessity of
inventing his characters. Among the less
strictly autobiographical novels, *The Rainbow* holds the foremost place. The three pairs
of lovers through which the passional ocean
rises are sufficiently differentiated among each
other, and the novel stands easily with *Le
Sacre du Printemps* and the cloud snapshots
of Stieglitz among the creative modern docu-
ments. But the novels and books immediately
successive to these are not quite as satisfactory. *Women in Love* is harder of substance and style than its predecessors; but it is
also a little thinner, and the two women, the
mother-woman and the woman who fights the
man, are really aspects of the same person,
and not separate figures. It is obvious that

Lawrence realized that he was at a parting of
the ways, and that he had to become either
frankly autobiographical or frankly dramatic-
objective; but that in spite of an effort to solve
his conflict, he had not been successful. Each
work exhibits the intellectual power of him in
a state of further maturity; but not each work
exhibits a surer poethood. *Sea and Sar-
dinia,* in form a travel book, is an incomplete confession, a subjective novel with the
chief character left half-off the scene. The two
romances, *The Lost Girl* and *Aaron's Rod*
reveal in Lawrence disregard of his material; as though the effort to create an objectivity in the novel had cut him off subconsciously from much of his interest in
what he was about. The former becomes
characteristic of its author, despite much
rapid, brilliant writing, only in its last
chapters; and the latter irritates with its ex-
asperated prose. Indeed, Lawrence in *Aaron's
Rod* is unable to express himself through the
terms of his drama. The situations are rather
thinly felt; and we find the author reverting
to the strategy of incomplete novelists: making his characters mouth certain theories
which very obviously interest him more than

do the characters themselves. Even so good
a story as *The Fox,* which, small in scale though
it is, announces a more economical and con-
trolled manner of writing than any yet ex-
hibited by its author, is spoiled by the *fabula
docet* in theoretic form. It is therefore comprehensible that a great many people not ma-
liciously disposed toward Lawrence should
have gone about for a while blackly convinced
that the author's power was setting. And only
with *Studies in Classical American Literature* and *Kangaroo* have we gotten books
new-evident of the author's genius. But they
make it freshly plain. The delightfully mock-
ing manner of the essays half-covers a giant's
imaginative vision focussed on the American
continent. The novel, distinctly autobiographical in matter, has the rare component of
a movable everpresent center, and succeeds,
where *Aaron's Rod* met with failure, in
notating the disintegrating surface of contemporary life.

And a gratitude goes out from us toward
this writer greater perhaps than any we give to
any other of his time. He stands toward our
day much as Richard Wagner stood toward his
own; and Wagner was the artist personally

courageous enough, and sufficiently familiar
with his medium, to permit that in the
human being which out in nature creates the
winter and the spring, to take a shape. He
beat the rhythm for his age, and the truth of
life, the relationship of things which is different in every age and perhaps at every hour, was
given the opportunity to erect itself in other
breasts which heard. And Lawrence brings the
identical impulse to freedom once again. He
forces the system of relationships which has
to be said at this very moment, and unexpressed
prevents the daily intercourse, to come to light.
He holds the mirror up to men in their most
secret trouble. There must be folk in thousands who have been made to live more truly
through his work. Each book has been a tearing new experience. It is characteristic that
the angriest of the opposition to him has
broken from the archaic ranks of the romantic males and the cast-iron feminists. And it is
with Wagner and the other artists who have
beaten out the rhythm for their ages that D.
H. Lawrence must come permanently to rest:
one of those stars which, seen or lost to sight,
help hold the planet in its course.

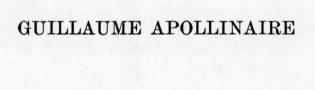

GUILLAUME APOLLINAIRE

GUILLAUME APOLLINAIRE

G UILLAUME APOLLINAIRE was a
playboy of the arts in metro'd electric
Paris. In the monster mechanical town of
wireless and elevators and nitrogen lamps and
placarded walls around the couchant Louvre,
he lived a kind of poetry. Possessed of a vo-
racious appetite for many kinds of experience,
a swift sensibility and an inextinguishable intellectual curiosity, he communicated his joys
and games and sensations not less through the
forms of ordinary existence than those of
literature. There are some writers who are
poets only in the secluded chamber, and in the
round of friendly contacts remain brown and
unlyrical like professors, intellectuals and
clerks. But Apollinaire was himself a fluid
and ambulant work of art. The most banal
manifestations of life, the casual business of
the day, got from him rhythm and glint. The
Apollinaire who stepped off a street-train or
opened a glass café-door or ate raviolis or
walked down a street in the Auteuil, was no

whit less exuberant, less lyrical, less imaginative than the one who sat before a writing table exuberantly molding words into poems and spinning capricious narratives. He was a magician in talk, enchanting folk with stories and fabrications in the café-corner or in the living-room. In the trenches, under the falling projectiles, he told tales, and got himself with the soldiers of his corps a reputation of entertainer like the one he sported in art-radical Paris. A letter to a friend, begun in playful prose, would suddenly under his hand lift into a poem; oftentimes a very finely articulated piece of verse. Like Mallarmé, but with greater spontaneity, he sent poems on post cards, in *petits bleus,* as dispatches. He was erudite, and he made his erudition play lightly along, and add a spice to the dish of life. He was, indeed, a created figure, a vivid and distinguished person, a somebody on the street.

The day must have been shot with brilliant beams, and the earth many vista'd and wide by the side of this charming cavalier of life. Men must have heard in the rhythm of his words the sound of their own inner voices, quite as in a play or poem. Men certainly caught gusto from him as combustible objects catch fire from

each other. Vast numbers of the ideas which
folk in Paris, and folk come here from Paris,
quite innocently sport as their own, were cast
upon the world first from the mouth of Apollinaire. Words which he spoke earnestly, and
words which he merely tossed cheekily about
like gay painted balls, alike were swallowed
hot. Who can say how much of the mind of
the most abandoned and reckless dada is a
creation of Guillaume Kostrowitsky's? An
art equally true on the plane of dream and the
plane of actuality,—who adumbrated it before
him? And during Apollinaire's last year,
when he transported about Paris a poetical
and military glory, a wounded skull and a body
somewhat too tightly draped in a spiffy new
uniform, he had a sort of court, a train in
which neither purple-necked ladies nor cul-
tural bounders, poets or eunuchs, experimenters in the arts and pseudo-people, were entirely unrepresented. For these parched souls
he did his verbal miracles, and made his feast
of *petits pains*. Time must indeed have moved
very languidly for many folk after the dreary
day when Apollinaire fell victim to the black
flu of 1918.

It was no long hair and velveteen coat, no

vie de Bohême and picturesque untidiness of
Montmartre that Apollinaire needed to make
this rich art of living for himself. Nor did
he require, as requires d'Annunzio, so that
life will flame about him, Renaissance magnificence, lordly quinquecento houses, horses,
hounds and airplanes, Greek Nikes extending
over the foot of luxurious beds the conqueror's
bays, orations to the populace upon the Capitoline. He kept the gemlike lights playing in
the ordinary sack coat and soldier's uniform;
for, set in the rim of his straw hat or soldier's
cap, resplended the precious stone that sat in
Tytyl's bonnet. Apollinaire had the power of
amusing himself. He had the gift of procur-
ing for himself aristocratic pleasures among
the ordinary house-walls and in the ordinary
paths of urban life. But had it been New York
where he lived and not Paris, he would no less
in this heavy place have found spots to eat
and drink and laugh and talk and see and
dream, or have invented them. For he had
gusto; and so, he dragged the sand of Paris
for its nuggets of ore and found its strange,
amusing, and noteworthy gold. He knew
places where Balzac had lived or Canudo slept
or Ernest La Jeunesse kept a collection of

watches in a chamber; knew odd corners and odd persons that were pleasant to see; knew where a chemical landscape was to be glimpsed from this friend's windows, or a witty old man to be met in this tiny bookshop on the left bank among elaborately bound pornographies, or a good dinner to be eaten in the cellar of the shop of a picture dealer, beneath Cézannes, without gravy of art-talk. He knew that on the corner of the boulevard there was a café where there were still boulevardiers of the classic cut, and that in such and such a street stood a wall inscribed with amazing phrases and designs. There was the pleasure of delicious dishes of food; and Apollinaire knew where to find it or how to prepare it himself; he was Epicurus' owne son, and his wife was assistant cook, only, in their apartment. There was the pleasure of a long fight for the appreciation of the work of the cubists; the friends of Wagner had not waged the only glorious battle for an art; there were new ones as glorious to be fought. And there were other pleasures to be had, or if there were no others, there were some to be invented by clever men. Did he not write:

Et puis, je ne crains pas la mort,
Mais bien l'emmerdement, c'est pire.

He knew a thousand curious things set down
in books; in the volumes that were hidden away
in the department of the National Library
called the Hell; in tomes dealing with the religions and history of the Mormons, or with
obscure heresies; in old chap-books recounting the adventures and the appearances of the
wandering Jew or the life and crimes of
Schinderhannes; in books of superstitions and
books of ballads; and he gobbled them all with
the gourmandise of a man cramming himself
with little cakes and cream-tarts. But the
stone in his hat turned of itself, too, and gave
him new sensations, new clues to new musics
and new fantasies. In the stones of Paris, and
in the jumbled world there was an illimitable
amount of objects exciting to the imagination.
Sensations gave style to the contents of his
mind. Sensations led to orientation on cubism;
cubism led to investigation of more accurate
means of representation; these speculations led
back again to his own breast and made him
hear the whirring of his own nerves more distinctly. All manner of common objects shot
illuminations onto each other. The dresses,

boas and hats in a milliner's window could make this man ponder on the shrinking rôle of the poet in modern life. An airplane rising through cloudlands might evoke a childish dream of Christ ascending bannered through the blue. The cravat binding his neck might call to mind the habits of thought which choke modern life. An Ingersoll might make him perceive the round of the hours of his own life; five o'clock and the poetry of the moment when the tea is poured and the taxi stops before the doorway down below.

And the marvelous pervasive gusto became of course the capacity for returning it again into the world through his medium. At their best his prose and poetry and criticism sparkle and dance with the alerted senses and nourished state which gave them birth; and at their least felt, contain an infectious playfulness and irresponsibility. Verse and tales are drunken and a little riotous with cerebral intoxication, and effervescent with a cleverness sometimes profound to the point of genius. Apollinaire plays with ideas and tosses drunken fancies; scatters little jewels of wit and erudition through pot-boilers; pictures Isaac Lequedem the Wandering Jew for a while and then the

Ludwig II of peasant tradition; makes of the
account of a promenade up a suburban street
a romance of adventure. "An art of foot-
notes," Mr. Josephson has called his prose.
Sensations, metaphors, colors drawn from a
half dozen fields of experience shoot through
his work. For his device he chose the words
J'emerveille, and he was indeed a sort of en-
chanter; not too scrupulous an artist; a little
facile at his best and given to momentary and
dramatic insincerities; but startling and dazzling with vivacity of mind. One feels the con-
jurer, especially in the more capricious portions of his stories; the wild and absurd excursions of fancy in *Le poète assassiné* and *La
femme assise,* with their marvelous descriptions of impossible robes made of feathers,
mirrors, live birds; of impossible machines for
suppressing time and space, of impossible religious crowd-ecstasies and impossible banquets and ceremonies among the Mormons.
There is the most delicious of flavors in his descriptions of the *bohême* in the Montparnasse
district before the war, made in the course of
Le femme assise. All the nostalgia for the old
ways and the café de la Rotonde which must
have assailed poor Apollinaire in the trenches

is squeezed into those bright pages with their description of the costumes of the DeLaunay pair at Bullier and of the line and repartee of the *debardeurs* at the opera ball; and into the sly notes on *"cette vie qu'animaient l'art, l'amour, la danse à Bullier et le cinéma,"* scattered through all the amazing and dislocated prose. Remarks about a street in Auteuil, about public libraries seen in various cities, Petrograd, Neuchatel, New York, about the origin of certain superstitions among soldiers, quite dryly made, nevertheless thrill one as a story might. And styles are juggled, three or four in *La femme assise;* and drunken ribald comments passed, in *Le poète assassiné,* on the state of the arts in the years before the war; scenes of drinking and wenching set down with light and Rabelaisian gusto; a whole showcase of surprising and merry things.

His literary invention, calligrammatic poetry, reveals best the man's awakenedness to the materials in his environment, and his researchful and experimental attitude on life. In this form, Apollinaire was attempting to make the medium of print itself become part of the communication of the written word. From everything in the world he got sensations; from the blocks of print in books and newspapers, too; and it suddenly had come to him that the spaces on the page, the black and white of letters and paper, might be made expressive, also. The verbal image is a notoriously feeble one. The poet is under a handicap when competing with painter or musician in the rendering of a sensation; for he has to rely largely on memory, which is pale; the clang of words themselves is not strong; while painter and musician act directly and freshly on the retina and the ear-drum. So Apollinaire decided to assist the verbal image by one actually pictured by the array of print. *Anch'io son pittore* flew the flags; he began composing sorts of half poems, half pictures. A poem about rain was printed to represent the long streaks of rain-water pouring down the sky to earth; a poem about a watch represented a watch; one about a cravat was arranged as a picture of a necktie. Of course, the idea did not originate entirely with Apollinaire. If one turns over a volume of the poems of old George Herbert, one will find certain of the ritualistic pieces, *The Table* for example, printed as "calligrammes." Baroque age always calls to baroque age. And Mallarmé,

in *Le coup de dés,* played with the space left by
the printed words, striving to use it. Nor was
Apollinaire entirely successful in his experiment. There is no doubt that the difficulty
of reading the words arranged in zigzags and
spirals takes away a great deal of the pleasure
given by the form. Apollinaire, too, seemed to
realize that only certain poems lent themselves
to the calligramme; he himself to the end composed lyrics in regular and in free verse, as
well as in the semi-pictural form. Still, the
idea has been developed by other poets, by Cocteau, Blaise Cendrars and by some of the
younger Europeans and Americans, and there
is no doubt the next decades will see literature
making increased use of the ready ally indicated to it.

There was a fighter in Apollinaire; he had
the communal feeling strongly developed. Not
the least important expression of his life consisted in combat for ideas. Particularly effective was the critical service done the cause of
cubism by him. If the gradual attunement of
the Parisian public to the new expressionistic
art is to be referred to the championship of any
one writer, it is to Apollinaire that the thanks
must go. He was a man of ideas with a back-

ground of practical living; and the men who
have taken up his pen, Cocteau for example,
are far more singly æsthetes than ever he was.
He took it upon himself to gain recognition for
the unpopular group around Picasso, and in
journal columns and a pamphlet he expounded
and defended and acclaimed the leader and
Rousseau, Braque, Picabia, Metzinger, the
Duchamp-Villon trinity, Gleize, Gris and
Marie Laurencin. No doubt, he was being quite
deliberately used by those interested in the
advancement of their own affairs, but in all
probability he was quite aware of the machina-
tion; perfectly content, indeed, to serve individual interests so long as a general cause
which impassioned him was furthered. And,
certainly, the interchange of thought which set
up between Apollinaire and Picasso and Picabia and Laurencin and the rest of the revolutionary painters, an interchange partly
literary, mostly oral, was active in the development of the aesthetic of the new art. In making clear to himself his own relation to the
canvases of the experimenters, and in ascertaining the principles of his comprehension of
them, the writer helped erect the philosophical
superstructure on these more lyrical and emo-

ability of the born poet. He would have synchronized with vital rhythm whether the hour had been spacious, calm and slow, or, as was that of Paris in the age of the war, hectic, weary and shrill. In any environment, in Athens or New York, in jail or in a Ceylonese jungle, he would in some fashion have succeeded in making himself an integral portion of what was moving; pierced, with the aid of imagination, the local crust, attained the universal, and satisfied an inborn need for harmony. No preconception of what the poet's life should be; no particular worry whether what he was doing in his day was at all related and commensurable with what Isaiah had done in his, or Greco or Cézanne or Beethoven in theirs, would have stopped him and hampered him and made him change his mind. What he would have been and what he would have done would doubtless have taken on the timbre of an age, and been different from the stuffs made in any other time. But they would also have spoken to all other times, and revealed, no matter how slight their proper weight, times to each other and a time to itself.

It is possible that Apollinaire has more chance of surviving as a figure, a saint of

literary men, than as an artist. He died too
young; he was a soldier and badly wounded
during the last best years of his life; and he
remained until the end always more the exuberant sporter with ideas and sensations, and
the fighter for new conceptions of art and
poetry, than the sustained literary creator.
The man of sensations and the curious intellectual were too rarely fused in the state of
feeling. Sensuous alertness was a great virtue in him: the life of the senses, inimical to
the past and the present and to convictions and
formulas. He stretched a new nervous surface
to the industrial landscape and the business of
the world, and claimed the new components of
nature, machines and placards and scientific
discoveries as the stuff of poetry. He wanted
for the poet the new universe of scientific,
microscopic, telescopic, radiographic vision;
for the poet the courage to leave accepted logic
for new untried chains of relations; for the
singer the compression of business language
and the rapidity of business thought. He himself was eternally occupied in clearing from
between himself and the external stimuli all
preconceptions, all rationalizing tendencies of

mind. And a kind of sounding sensorium he did become. The style of his inspired poetry does not contradict the style of the external gesture of our life. But there was a deeper tide which should have floated him, and used the vibrations of his epidermis in service to some great expression. And that tide did not come up in great extended roll, and lift his words. Something in himself remained untouched, or touched but little. There appears to have been a poetic Apollinaire who never quite managed to get himself out on paper and who remained unknown to all but a few persons. Externality, cleverness, mediocrity of means limits the effectiveness of most of his stories. Some of his writing it is true was frankly hackwork: *La fin de Babylon* for instance, done for an editor who owned some illustrations which he was eager to use, and required a text. But there were other pieces of fiction on which Apollinaire laid some store: *Le poète assassiné* and *L'heresiarche et Cie.;* and they, precisely because of the absence of a kind of intensity and feeling stand far inferior to the philosophic fantasies of Voltaire and Anatole France and de Gourmont, place beside

which they solicit. A similar tenuosity makes
much of his poetry ring not quite roundly: the
poems in the volume *Alcools,* in particular.
They are Appollinaire's, it is not to be questioned; for each of them confesses itself the
work of a man whose hand was singularly
fortunate, to whose touch all sorts of materials
responded, and who seems to have been able to
accomplish what he set out to do with a certain
smiling ease. Yet many of them despite their
happiness want just the sort of stylistic distinction which work of the first water
has. The examples of other poets and other
poetry seem to have haunted Apollinaire. One
cannot help remembering the Verlaine of
Fêtes Galantes in *Crèpuscule,* or the early
Mallarmé in *Le vent nocturne* and *Claire de
lune.* In *Rhenanes,* he trespassed upon the
territory of Heine; but he wanted naïveté; and
his *Loreley* is wooden, and *Schinderhannes*
merely gives a French equivalent for the bitter-
parodistic turns of the German poet.

Apollinaire's most substantial achievements
are the witty little poems of *Le Bestaire,*
and certain of the poems of *Calligrammes*
not printed in the form of pictures. In these

latter pieces, among which *Les Fenètres, Les Collines, Le Musician de Saint-Merry, Un Fantôme des Nuées* and *Vers Le Sud* are eminent, the words used arbitrarily and away from their accepted significance in the language, the abstract metaphors, the rapid brusque descriptions and the resemblances in sound which replace rhyme, and other elements which have become characteristic of modern poetry, are organic, pulsant with the mental excitement and lyric state which gave them birth. Hence Appollinaire has some likelihood of speaking his own hectic, shattered age to attentive men. His writings are like clothes that retain the aroma of cigars long since turned to ashes. Other times are like to see again in bits of Appollinaire the mind of literary men in a day which seemed unneedful of them, and found in the scientific men its priests. Or, they will sense in the really beautiful war-poems of *Calligrammes* the spirits of the soldiers who went eyes open into the battle: first, the chivalresque attitude:

> J'en ai pris mon parti Rouveyre
> Et monté sur mon grand cheval
> Je vais bientôt partir en guerre
> Sans pitié chaste et l'œil sévère

Comme ces guerriers qu'Epinal
Vendait Images populaires
Que Georgin gravait dans les bois
Ou sont-ils ces beaux militaires
Soldats passés.   Où sont les guerres
Où sont les guerrès d'autrefois. ;

then, the years of:

Ulysse que de jours pour rentrer dans Ithaque;

last, the complete pyrrhonism of *La femme assise,* the state of those who have acquiesced in a hated task and found themselves believing in consequence that nothing is of any importance, that all facts are equally trivial and unrelated, and not all the world worth a moment of intensity.   Besides, we cannot doubt it, these writings are certain of bringing to some readers the glamour of a life of letters enormously enjoyed, a life of letters danced rather more than mourned through.   Then, there will define itself again for a moment the stout radiant figure of Guillaume Apollinaire as he was when he flaunted the banner of cubism, and let his drunken fancy reel rather more than note facts down laboriously; and hectographed poems behind the lines, and led his cortege of desirous ones through the boulevards.   There will sing again for a moment a poem of the sort of the best of poems; a life lived out, a human figure irradiated by imagination, a chestnut flowering in asphalt among city cubes.

WALDO FRANK

WALDO FRANK

NOT any composition of Waldo Frank's, critical or narrative, leaves one unconscious of the vigorousness of his gift. Pages of his work offer to place him among the living inventors of English prose. Neither his master D. H. Lawrence, nor Joyce, Richardson, Cummings, nor any other modern stylist, possesses a talent for verbal orchestration essentially richer than his. Frank in instances models in hot color. Specially sensitive to the violence, weight and detonation of words; apprehending, apparently, their qualities and edges as with the naked flesh, he succeeds in embodying certain of his ideas and images in dense and living verbal matter. Scenes are conjured before the eye not alone by an appeal to memory. Resonances intuitively selected, arranged and contrasted transfer sensations directly to the ear; achieve the immediate, poetic communication. None of his novels is without passages streaming thick like tropic currents, and churned by racial vehemence,

city counter-rhythms, difficult voluptuousness.
Few of his stories stand entirely bare of solidly
architectured, sensuous paragraphs. Occasionally no more than a phrase or sentence exhibits
amid much dun and tasteless matter the touch
of the warm hand; upon some page of each
of his pieces, nevertheless, the garnet gleams,
and brings incontrovertible tidings of natural
brilliancies.

Frank has at times achieved expressive
form. Pages of intellectualized melodrama
wash idly by; suddenly, a scene, a mood, a
person moves in city street or country road
large and eternal underneath the dome; and
experiences shadowy and secret hitherto in the
fugitive modern psyche stand solid and memor-
able. Not many writers have rendered as
poignantly as Frank the moments when life
casts from the depths her blackest word, and
the harsh music of destiny is clear and level
above the defeated soul. He has caught
directly the half-audible music everlastingly
wailing its gamuts up and down the Jewish
heart, and the clear acrid air of release from
half-genuine erotic episodes. Cloud's stilly
thunderous emotions in the hostile street of
white men, and Cloud's bodily relaxation in

green gulf water; the contrasting qualities of
vitality, of smell, even about the persons of
the two neighborly women, the one fecund the
other barren; the sensation of the neurotic lad
sent for the first time to sleep with an
elder brother, are truly, finally seen. *Our
America* contains critical formulations and
appraisements of the American situation profound and scarcely to be improved upon.

With perfect justice Frank has attempted
carrying the substance of the novel into the
field of abstraction. Since writing *Sons and
Lovers,* D. H. Lawrence has stressed the projections of the subconscious mind, the voices
of the earth behind the intellect; and used as
subject matter the invisible magic lanterns
which cast the visions of his protagonists upon
the empty screen of the world. Jules Romains,
Frank's other living influence, pictures the
spirits of groups and hours possessing themselves of individuals, and seeing, speaking, acting, through them. But the youthful New
Yorker has focussed his attention more directly than either of these novelists have done
upon the hidden ground-movements of the
psyche. In his novels and tales, the plane of
the concealed motors and projectors of percep-

tion becomes the immediate foreground. Characters are expressed through sharpest qualification of what lies between them and the objects present to their senses. Personal projections are underlined, surfaces penetrated, half conscious rhythms broadly developed. The ever-waxing pre-occupation with abstractions has progressively individualized Frank's art. If the earliest of his novels, *The Unwelcome Man,* despite its lyrical strain, remained pretty definitely within the limits of reality established by the semi-autobiographical novel of the nineteen hundreds, the forms of both *The Dark Mother* and *Rahab* were conceived as flowing from the rhythm of an unconscious life. And latterly, Frank has daringly identified the subterranean stream of his protagonists with the pattern created by the subject-matter within himself, and let the form evolve directly from this subjective sense of pitch and flow. In intention, at least, the story-cycle *City Block,* and the novel *Holiday,* approach the condition of music.

Frank stands vigorous, aggressive, hot-blooded among American writers. If natural brilliance does constitute genius, then something of the wondrous principle may be said to

reside in him. The traits of the individual who
has set moving these solid tides of prose, and
constructed in theory, at least, as complicated
patterns of human relationships as those of
The Dark Mother and *Holiday,* must appear
substantial to every eye. The literary culture
and intellectual background involved in these
constructions would distinguish its possessor,
were he a Frenchman, in Lutece herself; and in
Manhattan such mental equipment towers.
Nevertheless, all of Frank's novels, despite
their grandiose attacks on form, pour forth,
with some clear orange flame, much chok-
ing sullen smoke. Momentarily manifest so
warmly, largely, compellingly, this lyrical
talent remains to a marked degree tangled
and unchanneled, exhibiting all the symtoms
of an incorrectly functioning vitality. In the
lengthy stretches that separate achieved passages, it either charges sporadically in clumsy
assaults upon effectiveness, or rebels, con-
tracts, and constricts itself like an element
driven in a direction unnatural to it, and into
a form distinctly not its own.

None of his more ambitious works exhibits
the direct and well-sustained application of the
intelligence to the materials of art. Even as

fluid and rich a piece of portraiture as *Under
the Dome, aleph,* is incomplete as a form, and
declarative of only half the picture; and *Our
America* stands a brilliant sketch. Certainly,
no work of his displays the wholeness and inevitability which pervade things come to pass
either out in the field of life or within the
imagination of the artist; and all, in their
formal dislocations, give evidence of having
been induced and prearranged and glued together by a theorizing intellect. It is the genius of D. H. Lawrence to throw again and
again organic fictions: *Sons and Lovers, The
Rainbow, Kangaroo;* natural, subtle, unrationalized counterpoints of unconscious and environment, of deeds and visions, a truth a
novel relations. But it is not Frank's.

The greater proportion of his work sounds
forced, false and "off." Ten, twenty and
thirty stalks at its rancidest in innumerable
conversations of his characters. It would seem
that all of them, with scarce an exception, from
the Tammany politician to the negro mammy
in her cabin, have but recently been to see the
melodrama, and adopted its insensitive accent
with utter conviction. The priest says "This
man has sucked me—what does he want?" Mr.

Kandro says "I have been true to my hurt."
And the woman who has just fornicated with
the priest says "I have something now to give
at last to my husband," without a comic
thought in her mind at all. To read one of
Frank's conversations after reading even the
dryest, most labored of his descriptions is to
be violently jounced from out a dream. But
the style of the narrative portions continually
runs off into writing almost equally sensational
and untrue. *Ce n'est point ainsi que parle
la nature.* Suddenly, after some throb-
bing, rich descriptions, the words like
characters in the melodrama draw pistols on
each other and explode them without provoca-
tion. Detail is perpetually given an exaggerated relief; without necessity immense Picas-
soesque strokes shoot out; the crude, the primitive, the powerful tones obtrude. Cups and
saucers yearn over each other as the mouths of
thirsting animals. *The Dark Mother,* like
Diana of the Ephesians, is full of breasts. But
a dissonance is apparent. The Picasso-like effects are inorganic, chiefly; and the breasts remind one not of flowers of flesh but of certain
deceptive articles of rubber (or is it cloth?),
said to be purchasable at drug stores. In jerk-

ing the reader constantly into attention to itself, the technique breaks the rhythm and suggests the presence of a vacuum.

With the exception of the little Jewish tailor in his shop and the woman in the candy store, scarcely one of Frank's characters is thoroughly consistent and convincing. The greater number are in two completely dislocated pieces: life of action and life of feeling. He is found continually violating the human nature. How many of his people could not turn upon Frank like the woman in *La Robe Rouge* upon the ambitious judge, and cry, *"d'un innocent vous avez faillè faire un forcat, et d'une honnête femme, vous faites une criminelle!"* The modes of apprehension, psychic ground planes and inward experiences of how many of them, are quite unrelated to what the author would have us believe, from their names, their races, their parents, their environments, their histories, to be their identities! The reactions of Quincy Burt in *The Unwelcome Man,* and those of the two heroes of *The Dark Mother,* David Markand and Tom Rennard, are undistinguishable. Quincy on Brooklyn Bridge and in the streets of New York on New Year's Eve, David in Wall and

Water streets, Tom aboard the Chicago-New York express, are shown endowed with exactly similar nervous systems. All three of them appear to come of the same race, to have had similar histories, similar opportunities, similar intellectual developments, emotional adventures, similar pains and resentments. Not only do they exhibit the general resemblance which men of a single generation, a single class, a single race and nation might be supposed to possess. The three of them, and, for that matter, Cornelia Rennard also, react as a single person. Quincy on Brooklyn Bridge overlooking Manhattan appears, to himself,

"to be looking down upon an illimitable graveyard. Each house was become a tomb-stone, each towering building, in the light of day a sentinel of progress, appeared now a monument to some great death.—The moiling tenements glowed forth like coral. Poverty, catching a deflected ray, turned lurid.—The waters were in shadow as if night had been an emanation from them, pushing the sun relentlessly back across the rim of the world. Above the harbor was a deep pall, night's advance guard in its grey, the sun's resistance in its orange fretting. The pall fell, and the waters grew more brackish. The sun plunged down through the mists, pouring a frenzy of disparted color that shot above the buildings of South Manhattan.''

On Wall Street, David Markand perceives ''Glass casements fronting heavy buildings, huge masonry pillared by slender stone—the grass and loom, the hypocrisy of Power. Spawn of the buildings: men with naked singing nerves like wires in storm, and women with dead eyes, women with soft breasts against a hard tiding world. Furious streets. A street wide and delirious with men waving their straw hats like banners. Streets narrow and somber that curled like smoke across the feet. Streets eaten with secret moods. Streets cluttered and twisting with pent power. Streets pulsant like hose. Streets slumberous like pythons. Streets writhing and locked. A wide gash of sky. The sun was a stranger. The blue was a burn. —David—walked toward his uncle's office that was to swallow him up. Walked down to where it waited him, a block from Wall Street. Life was sea-yearning. Shops sold sails and compasses and binnacles. In the smart of the salt a scent and a sense of spices. Coffee and wines were at home here in the grime of the North, had brought with them the linger of their homes. Tobacco. Musty housings for jagged yellow leaves. A brooding, reeking, murmurous street.—David fell down the funnel of a world. The waters touched him that touched far lands. Pregnant waters.''

And the sensations of Tom Rennard the young lawyer, the future politician, are of a color, a character, not at all different. As the train swung him ''southward from Chicago about the duned neck of the Lake,'' he has a vision of the town of his childhood. And for him ''The train was swimming up the path of the sun. The world cut flat from the train's stride like a sea from the prow of a racing vessel. The horizon swayingly scooped: trees low and faint in the shrill sky, nude in young leaves, lascivious in blossoms, almost bowled over by the roll of the world—and the blue belch of sturdier chimneys beyond, scattered half-acres of hell spewing soot and shadow over a scarred and flowered prairie. In his eyes an old sick town—. The long street swooned under foliage. Trees crowded between the two rows of houses as if they had burst them apart. Under the arrogant verdure the little wooden

boxes of men crouched and were smothered. A
man came out from the dull pressure; he
walked into the sway of the trees: he went forth
to his toil: he was immersed in the redundance
of fields.''

Indeed, it would be possible to assign, arbitrarily, the gorgeous sensations of any one of
these youths to any other, without disturbing
the drawing. One could put David on Brooklyn Bridge and let him see what Quincy saw
without committing a vandalism, make Tom
Rennard see Wall and Water streets with
David's eyes, imagine Quincy both ''falling
down the funnel of a world'' on the East River
front of Manhattan, and perceiving the street
of his native village of Harriet, Long Island,
''swooning under foliage.'' What is more, one
could even manage to place any one of the three
youths in the situation of Cornelia in the chapter which describes the Thanksgiving Day
morning of that shadowy sister of the Alissa of
Gide, and attribute to him, without excessive
adaptation, the experiences described there.
But although the reactions of Quincy, David,
Tom, and Cornelia are the reactions of a single
person, that person, it is scarcely necessary to

point out, is neither a boy named Burt born
into an unintellectual family in Harriet, Long
Island, a boy named Markand fresh from a
bicycle repair shop in central New York, a
young lawyer and future politician, nor a
sculptress fugitive from paternal puritanism.
These complex emotions, states of depression,
lyrical exaltations, are charged with a personality in nowise plotted by the data with
which Frank has sought to limn his characters.
Could David have felt in the manner indicated
by the author, he most certainly would not have
done what Frank assures us he did, remained
in his uncle's tobacco business and found advancement in it. He would have departed immediately for Paris and sat waiting for
Marinetti to join him. But it is not possible
that he could have felt with those particular
nuances of feeling. For in order that he
should be able to do so, there would have had
to be circulating in his veins a blood entirely
other than that supposedly his. Behind the
person who could feel as Frank's protagonists
are said to feel, there must have been lying
an experience entirely other than that pre-
sumed by the author. The accents, the nuances
of these sensations, refer to a mentality very

richly endowed with a special faculty for dramatizing life and making literature.

Acute dislocation exists likewise in the personages of Frank's more recent novels. It is merely less obvious for the reason that the author has situated himself definitely within the protagonists, and identified life with their visions of it. Nevertheless, the characters never quite justify the emotions he seeks to rouse in us for them. The fact that all are rationalizers, consistently disguising the truth of their feelings from themselves and over-busied explaining everything they do, does not ground our quarrel with the story-teller. What does constitute it, is the fact that he himself is deceived by their rationalizing habits of mind, accepts them as truthful, and strives to convert us to his point of view. So many of his people belong to the type of those whose vanity causes them to feel that all things ought to be done for them, and who stand ever eager to prove the heavens guilty of crime against them; and Frank would have us see in them martyrs to the cruel caprice of life. Rahab, the mistress of a house of assignation, very patently a person with no sexual will of her own and submissive to all wills directed against her, the aban-

doner of her baby, a sentimentalist full of self-
pity, he seeks to palm off upon us as a saint. In
collapsing into shabby shadows, she "falls
toward God," he claims; and points to St.
Theresa who knew that God was in all things.
But even if we accept the unrealistic terminol-
ogy in which the author indulges himself, it
nevertheless remains impossible for us not to
wonder whether the Spanish agonist or any
other vital mind of the day when talking about
"God" was not obsolescent, would have
shared in Frank's curious incapacity. Would
they had failed to distinguish creatures with
over-swollen conceit, masochistic tendencies
and generally neurotic characteristics from
those as realistic in their acceptance of pain,
defeat and death as martyrs are; or shown as
great a readiness to feel, as he has done, a
whole in half a picture? We cannot believe
them so naïve.

Even when Frank abandons all effort to
individualize his characters by realistic methods, and accepts them merely as modes of racial
substance, he proves himself equally incapable
of creating consistent and convincing norms.
Holiday remains a brilliant fantasy, rhyth-
mical, full of melody and lush color, but ex-

pressive of no reality outward or inward, and unthinkable in any sense as a representation of the South. And, since the book gives the freest and least forced of Frank's writings, it relieves in greater sharpness his limitations as a novelist and as an artist. We have finally to recognize that, despite his boldness of attack, he wants the artist's healthy humility before the materials of his art, wants respect for the identity of the substance before him, and perfect readiness to throw aside all preconceptions for the purpose of approximating more closely the shape of the thing which exists. He will not open himself to objects or feelings sufficiently long, it appears, to give them the opportunity of declaring themselves in all their own natural fulness. The attitude in which we find him indulging himself is that of an insolence in the face of life. A look or two has sufficed him; he has gotten of them what his purpose required; the door has slammed; and he is imperially prepared to demonstrate with violence that his picture of a feeling, of a man, a woman, the American South or an East Side block, Spain, Spinoza or the conversational quality of simple people is an accurate one.

Erudite, powerful, brilliant, he stands in the limbo of the literary rationalizers; he has quit it episodically only. Frank is unconsciously impelled, it appears, into the making of fantasies. He cannot touch life quite nudely; he must have preconceptions about it. Like so many of his personages, he is interested more than he knows in proving life guilty of a special malice. He approaches his material with the unconfessed wish of making it substantiate his thesis, and forces the protective machinery of a convenient apriorism, a plot or metaphysical formula upon his unconscious life. The changes on the idea "to be beautiful, particularly in America, is to be damned" have been rung in one after another of his books and, because of Frank's literary culture and intellectual development, been expressed with great adroitness. *The Unwelcome Man* sets forth to paint the destruction of a sensitive spirit at the hands of a stupid family and a brutal world; the story suggests that the sensitive and lovely are unwelcome underneath the sky. In *The Dark Mother* the country was to be given its history of a noble generation uprooted and "condemned" to mediocrity and failure. *Our America* showed him obsessed with the conception of the "defeated Jew." *Rahab* seems to be a sort of perverse theodicy, apologetic for God the cruel lover pressing his favorites downward in the world and embracing them in the slime. *Holiday* pictures two people passionate for one another and forced by a social conflict into becoming, one the butcher, the other the victim. And, persuaded of the reality of these hypochondriac imaginations, and blindly compelled to gain credence for them among others, Frank is perpetually pressed to do violence to the nature of his gift. His observations are submitted to the Procustes-bed of preconceptions fortified by allegedly Freudian, Jungian, Spinozistic and unanimistic theory. Unimportant detail and external motives are overplayed in the attempt to compensate for want of a strong intuitive grasp upon human motive; and large bold showy strokes called up to mask the feeling of insecurity; until the author's travail occupies the forefront of the stage. In order to rationalize fantastic melodrama, Frank has squandered treasuries of verbal orchestration, colored descriptions, lyrical movements, psychological niceties. But under the elaborate surface the wires rasp. The sensational

detail does not make good the want of intuitive
relation with life; and the character-disorgan-
izations grate. Strange, that at times insur-
mountable barriers should seem to oppose
themselves to the confession of a simple
truth, and make it easier to pile Cézan-
nesque Pelion on Ossa, erect the complicated
edifice of a not quite ingenuous mysticism, and
indulge in embraces of the Godhead and visits
with the Absolute, than to avow in holy, painful candor that way to the embrace of man is
closed, and profoundest loneliness the portion!

It is possible that Frank, once freed of the
necessity of making fantasies, might nevertheless continue in the dramatic objective form,
and build on the foundation, lain by Lawrence's psychic explorations. *City Block*
shows him at intervals near success with it,
and it might veritably prove his medium. And
yet, we find ourselves suspecting that an uninhibited play of his peculiar intelligence on the
materials of life would turn him away from
the novel, and set him to work in the frankly
subjective and critical forms. Despite his momentary success with the objective manner,
he seems to us very distinctly a lyric poet
and a theoretical intelligence who because

of a fundamental maladjustment has been seeking to function in a direction contrary to the one naturally his own. He spreads an extraordinarily receptive sensorium to the moods of nature in city and field. He has a rich instrument with which to measure the quality of subtle, wayward personal states. Would not the "I, Walt Whitman" type of free, personal rhapsody enable him to unite in a form his very respectable talents? Besides, no novel of his has contained even a moiety of the interest and variety to be found in *Our America*. It is the analytical power in Frank which, more, even, than his spirit of daring and of infectious self-confidence has exercised the great beneficial influence on the members of the last two upsprouting generations in America, and placed many struggling talents in his debt. Even if *Salvos* reveals him most unattractively off-hand, all of his critical prose makes one to cry for more.

Indeed, it seems very possible that in these two fields, slighted by Frank and neglected for a third, his kingdom lies. Yet, whether actually it does; or whether Frank was born indeed for the novel, it may be we shall never come quite certainly to know. Decision would flow only from an uninhibited free experience with subject matter. And it is precisely an experience of the material of life that, up to the present writing, Frank has appeared incapable of undergoing in any generous measure.

MARCEL PROUST

MARCEL PROUST

NOVEL-WRITING for Marcel Proust was patently the means of quelling a destructive internal conflict. His work, unlike the writings of many other romancers, does not conceal this mechanism and offers it very simply to the eye. We are given to see that, in the sphere of action, experiences already lived and experiences still awaiting him wrestled for the author's interest, and that neither could abidingly compel it. The past was perpetually awash over the man. The title of his dreamy prose, *A la recherche du temps perdu,* informs us so. He himself, in the first pages of the first of the many books, shows us in what manner his libido streamed backward toward the monuments of his past days, investing them with a soft glamour nothing before him would take. For his protagonist and Proust are one; the fiction is a tri-dimensionalized representation of his own mundane career. And the desire in him to permit what had already developed out of him to remain unmodified; the

desire to refuse all new contact, was so powerfully organized in the man that, awakening
suddenly from sleep many nights, he would
perceive, where he had left the familiar furniture of his bedroom when he dozed, not the
objects themselves but the trappings of rooms
long since inhabited by him and long since quit.
In that swooning moment it would be the room
of a country-house, occupied in boyhood, that
lay about him again. Or, it might be a chamber, inhabited at some coast resort during the
time when he lived in the shadow of young
girls in bloom; or one known when he watched
for the red slippers of a Duchess before her
door, and penetrated ever more remotely into
the mysterious and stuffy recesses in which
move, as deep sea fish in their element, prin-
cesses and royal highnesses and Coburgs.

Time passed loudly clicking before the
mirage faded and left him knowing the objects
present to his senses. And to Proust, it was as
though the complex of associations, suddenly
evaded from the unconsciousness, were lodged
in certain portions of his own body. It was
the portion of his past, stored in the side of
his frame against which pressed the resistant
bedding that had claimed him; the past

through which moved the image of the elegant M. Swann, friend of the Prince of Wales and of the Comte de Paris; or that associated with the exploration of the occult regions of the Faubourg St. Germain. It was, indeed, his own person which had captured his attention, and offered him a banquet which none of the beings near him now could rival. And oftentimes, he tells us, after one of these sudden references to the past, he would lie awake all the night, plunging deep into his memories as persons to whom the world is too cruel do; sifting through his mind in slow, sweet revery the many pictures that follow each other after the sudden orientation onto past experience, touching his souvenirs as women bereaved of babies handle the cap and socks and bib worn by the dead infant, or as lonely persons read and re-read and read over again and again love-letters sent them years since, or as old men perceive and recount very plainly just how it was that their grandmothers handed pennies to beggars and fell asleep on the sofa after dinner.

But there existed a life in Proust that would not consent in this passive fondling of memories. It was fresh underneath the malady and

weariness and disillusionment, dashing itself
against the fixation of interest in the past. It
desired to have relation with what lay about
it, to develop itself through manipulation of
materials. The ritual of the neurasthenic could
not satisfy it. Crises and symptoms and mental agonies could not debauch it entirely. It
struggled out toward people; it filled anew
the man with dream and desire and hope. The
excessive capacity for feeling, the excessive
sensitiveness to people and to objects and to
states of external nature, had increased with
the passage of time, and made it imperative for
the man to make responses to the world about
him, to associate himself with the existing fact.

A vast wisdom had come to him through his
adventures with people; and needed to be ap-
plied. Neurasthenia had perhaps given him
insight of a sort which better-adjusted folk do
not have opportunity to acquire. Himself the
victim of the atrocity of nerves, alternately
shaken and bewitched by circumstances that
only mildly affect others, subject to emotional
storms which seem the results of external
stimuli and have indeed very little affair with
the innocent pegs onto which they are hung, he
had been forced to take notice of the gigantic

rôle played by the unconscious in ordinary affairs. Freud is by no means a sport in this
time. He is a portion of the central Zeitgeist
of an age which has begun to perceive that the
passions, too, have their rationale. For Freud
is just commencing to become known to
France; Proust's work was well begun before
1914; and yet this Frenchman saw behind the
scenes of life in much the manner which is
dubbed Freudian. He perceived to what a degree all that ever happens to us, all the understanding of the events in which we have taken
part, our whole picture of the universe, indeed,
is willed by the forces seated in our flesh. Sensations, emotions, all the crystallizations of
love and of aversion, they became for Proust
merely darts of light on a stilly flowing stream,
wave-caps cast up and annihilated again by a
silently rolling ocean. Underneath sensations
of beauty and spasms of love, underneath
dreams and fancies and illusions, he saw the
hidden forces of life, not the general mythological "will" seen by the elder idealist, but
animal hunger and sexual desire and pride;
saw them through "consciousness," preparing
the organism for some aggression willed by
them. He knew what folk without insight,

what the modish young men and perverse wilful women amid whom he moved did not suspect, that we invest each other imaginatively
with our own qualities, and adore in each other
an image which we ourselves project.

The world, the objects in his Paris apartment and in the country about the ancestral
house, and in Venice and Cabourg, here revealed to him merely the fleeting lights which
haunt slumber. They, too, were perceived sudden crystallizations, like love and hatred, of
the appetites; neutral objects suddenly played
upon by lights from his unconscious, and become precious for some obscure reason of life.
All he had come to know of people, of his rela-
tives, of doctors, dukes, servants, ambassadors,
of his mistresses, in truth, was only what
his being wished to know of them, could bear
to know for the sake of balance; was what was
pleasant for him to know, because it flattered
his self-conceit and his instinct for the preser-
vation of his life. It was all, this picture of
the world, even the churches he adored, and the
great swells he had known, and the crushes he
had developed, and the suffering he had undergone, the colors projected from a magic lantern
upon a white screen; and he was finally aware

that the reality was not the screen or the shifting images, but the lantern and the tinted slides that were projecting what his senses perceived. He came to listen, above the bustle of the senses, for the quietly flowing stream of life in him, whose play the universe visible to his senses was; for the movement of his being itself before it became expressively directed, and was only a dumb feeling and blind surge. There, he heard and saw formation and destruction, passion builded up like a castle and then demolished overnight again, colors and perfumes brewed for the skies and blossoms of the earth, banners painted that lead men to victories and death, a sorcerer's armory of mirages and joys and intoxications and despairs.

Neither of the two conflicting principles of Marcel Proust's existence were able to triumph. He could neither go mad nor live himself out through people, and he seems to have died before the ink was long dry on his last characters. But in the mysterious activity of art he was able to harmonize the two tugs. In the business of novel writing he suddenly found that it is possible to effect what he could not effect in the world of action; both relive the past, and experience anew. In the æsthetic process, the two, the fixation on the past and the appetite for renewed life, hitherto irreconcilable enemies, suddenly became allies, and supported each other contrapuntally. Both played along, quite amicably. The author was both handling his memories and straining at his bonds. The subject matter of *A la recherche du temps perdu* is, to be sure, quite as in the day dream, the past experience. During the writing, the author was once more in the worlds dropped behind him. A long inner soliloquy unfurled its prodigious length. Once again, he was the boy among the fine bourgeois in the old garden of Combray, the neurasthenic youth bathing at Balbec and seeing debutantes stroll past him with the movements of figures in a Greek frieze, the cool young climber into the salons of the Marquise de Villeparisis and of the Duchesse de Guermantes and of the Princesse de Guermantes-Bavière; and reliving every tingle of his nerves, every pleasure of his eyes and ears once vouchsafed him. Into the book he boldly poured his own story, his neurasthenia, his snobbery, his egocentricity. The characters are, very many of them, portraits of persons who figured saliently in the aristocratic society under the Third Republic; it is not only certain places, Cabourg, for example, that are recognizable under the names Proust has fancifully bestowed on them; persons part of the noble faubourg are said to have no difficulty in referring to their originals many of the brilliant character sketches which Proust has strewn with prodigal hand through his writings.

Nevertheless, the long revery of the author at his work-table was a preparation for new experience rather than a further laming. Proust, the mature man of the world was analyzing Proust, the young eremite of duchesses. He succeeded in accomplishing one of the most difficult of maneuvers. The book is as different from the autobiographical novel as we know it as it is from the conventional memoirs. Proust has treated himself as the stuff of fiction; detached himself and seen himself in three-dimensional perspective. Conscience came to him of his own blind-spot, as well as of the blind-spot of the men and women he contacts. It is well nigh the history of a libido, which is set before us. What Henry James sought all his days to do, to approfundize his own sensations, to explain why a certain place,

a certain person, a certain name, stirred him
as it did; and what James for some timorous-
ness was never quite able to do, that this nervous Parisian laboriously achieved. He was
reconstructing his own past in the light of the
acute self-knowledge he had gotten with living.
The neurasthenia was finally referred to the
source of mother-attachment. In recalling his
sensations, he was at the selfsame time stepping behind them and demonstrating their
causes, demonstrating the many separate
atoms which were crystallized into a dream, a
white night, a passion. Hence he gave us not
episodes, memories, portraits, but a sort of
incessant, flowing Maya-activity of budding
and wilting dreams, immense blooms of feeling
and romance, which started out of the flesh and
filled the cosmos with their hue and odor, then
dwindled again without reason and disappeared to make way for new, differently
colored and directed dreams. The succession
of these visions is, indeed, the stuff of this
novel. Great portions of the work are merely
the different facets of certain characters—
Swann, Odette, Saint-Loup, Albertine, M. de
Charlus, for example; for each person known
is but the revealer of a new facet of the old

self. Swann seen in the old garden at Combray among the people who will not believe, since he is known to them, and since they are quite simple and bourgeois, that he is part of the noble faubourg; Swann seen ruining himself socially for a cocotte, and sick with unrequited love; Swann dying, and in the stress of the *affaire* becoming the stubborn Jew again; these are three separate and superficially unrelated colors, which, juxtoposed, caused the movement of the eye. Such juxtapositions alone give one the sense of the passage of time, for the hero seems always of the same age, prematurely old. A major orientation is the one which takes place at the end of the last volume published at this time—a sudden discovery to the hero of the monstrous commerce in progress between M. de Charlus and Jupien, and a consequent penetration into the world of homosexuality. Several more such sudden turnings and confrontations are to be expected in the volumes yet to be issued; Proust had doubtlessly many new visions of Albertine, Ghisele, Odette and Saint-Loup to give before the history of his own development was completed.

Thus in the process of finding the past,

Proust was making his roundabout run for liberty. The search for time that was passed was with him, indeed, a rigorous appreciation of the past, a judgment of the value of the past, and, consequently, a stripping off of it of the purely irrational glamour with which the yearnful, nostalgic unconscious has invested it. In striving to recapture the departed years, the author, half-awarely, was attempting to remove his interests out of the region uncontrolled of the reason, and to place them in the clear light of day. For, once seen, once delimited and felt as with the fingers, whatever its beauty, whatever its irretrievable loveliness, time gone is perceived to be essentially like the present, to be of the same stuff that is afloat in the air today, and therefore not magical and full of the deity of the unknown. The *recherche du temps perdu* seems therefore to have been an attempt to give the present and the future the fair chance which the backward-flowing libido would deny to it.

The dense prose mass which has been set forth in the course of this process is a deep stilly moving tide. The nearly *maladif* refinement of his sensibilities, the depth of his psychological insight, has drawn forth from the granary of Proust's mind a stream of the most delicate and subtle detail, and this thick body of material moves in slow, noiseless, deep progression. Oftentimes the eddies are so large, the pages given over to the examination of a single point of psychology so many and so densely packed that one almost forgets in which direction the current is moving. For it is a profoundly sedentary prose which unrolls its slow languid stream through Proust's ten odd volumes. The writing contains the vital principle of its author, and he was a man lying abed, sleeping all day, writing all night, neurasthenic and afraid of noise: striving to limit his motor-activity and withhold himself from life. Hence, unconsciously, he lingered over moments and scenes, seeking to extract all the pleasure they contained, sucking them dry of every sensation to be gotten from them, before passing onward; and the curious invertebracy and wandering complexity of the sentences reveals a certain resistance to direction. Something of the dreaminess and vagueness of the writing of George Moore is in this style, too, although Proust wrote at once more journalistically and carelessly, and more finely and nervously than his Irish brother. The sentences

growing out of Proust's orchild-like malady
are almost singular in the museum of French
literature for their many-branchedness, their
capricious turns and drops and excursions. As
in the paintings of the cubists, the leaps of the
modern imagination across time and space, the
orientation on to many ages and modes and
scientific theories unites in this style many
different and clashing strands of experiences,
comma-barred in a single period. And Proust
drew his analogies and similies, which arose
in him with astonishing spontaneity, from
many regions of human exploration. He
seems to have learned from history and from
botany, and from art, as well as from human
intercourse. But his prose is for the greater
part quite anti-lyrical. The author gives himself rather more in the delicacy of his analyses,
in the wisdom of the reflections worked at frequent intervals into the body of his giant
soliloquy, than in any heaped-up sonorities or
grandiose colorations. Proust is one of the
great psychological instructors; it has been
said that one could gather a new LaRoche-
foucauld from this novel. And, certainly,
numerous, profound little essays on human
psychology, the wonderful and terrible one

with which the book *Sodome et Gomorrhe*
opens, for example, might with equal benefit
be extracted from its many pages.

With Proust, the novel of analysis, after
almost a century of quiescence, returns to the
center of the literary stage. The brothers De
Goncourt, Renan, perhaps even Ruskin, helped
make possible the subtle effects of this prose;
but the work of Proust itself touches hands
with the French novel which antedated Balzac
and the realistic orientation. The mid-nine-
teenth century form registered chiefly the external effects of passion. It represented with
infinite truth in what fashion people acted
under emotional stress. Balzac and Flaubert
knew with the greatest exactitude what people
did, what they said, how they appeared. But
it was rarely that they concerned themselves
with the manner of sensation of their characters. What goes on within, in what fashion
the stimulus is received, of what the emotions
themselves are composed, that did not occupy
them. The Russians, Dostoievsky in particular, may have situated the actions of their
novels largely in the minds of their characters,
and shown us the subjective world. The
French remained without; or, if they wished,

as did Flaubert in *La Tentation de Saint Antoine,* to represent the tragedy of thought, they pictured the mind, characteristically enough, in the form of hallucinatory vision. But with Proust there begins again the chain of those novelists whose interest is the complexity of the human heart. We are once more in the company of those who know how the intellect feels within; know the sensations of lovesickness and jealousy and of falling out of love; and have observed well the springing of the mind, the beating of the nerves. Your novelist of the eighteenth and commencing nineteenth centuries, there can be no question, would be perplexed, were he, in the Elysian fields, to be shown a copy of *A l'ombre des jeunes filles en fleur* or of *Le côté des Guermantes,* and told that this complex, capricious many-minded proseman was his heir-apparent. The orchid-like luxuriance of Proust's narrative is so very different from the soberer analyses of his forebears. But the fine French critics of the hour, M. Jacques Rivière, for instance, are able to perceive underneath the epidermic differences the blood-relationship, and will tell you no classic novelist has more fully obeyed the classic precept that the novel be "a discourse on the passions," than has this latter-day Parisian.

But it is not alone the analytical novel of an hundred years since which *A la recherche du temps perdu* resembles. This so modern history bears a likeness to a great piece of writing done two centuries ago. Of all books, it most recalls the memoirs of the Duc de Saint-Simon. Of imitation of any sort, there need be no question. Yet the whole range of the spectrum by no means separates the informal, full and occasionally archaic style of the courtier of Louis XIV and of the Regent d' Orleans from the sensuous, nervous phrases of the friend of Gaston Calmette and Leon Daudet. And there can be question but that Saint-Simon influenced considerably the outlook of Proust. It is comprehensible that the modern young devotee of French society should have found in this writer an instigator to an ideal distortion. A parody of the manner of the pride-mad duke was included in the set of witty burlesque of various authors published by Proust under the title of *Pastiches;* it requires no special gift to perceive from it how minutely Proust has felt the character behind the memoires, as he felt the characters behind

the writings of Flaubert and Renan and De
Regnier and the De Goncourts. It is even
highly probable that he had in mind Saint-
Simon when he attacked his own life for the
purposes of representation; for at the commencement of his work the talk in the garden
turns upon Saint-Simon, and Swann begins a
remark on the applicability of the observations
of the memoirist to certain aspects of mundane
life: a fact which might contain some indication for the reader of the between-the-lines.
The insertion of pen portraits of his great ones
into the body of his narrative certainly approaches Proust to the old memoir-writer of
the palace of Versailles; and the interest in
ceremonials was equally hypertrophied in
both.

What, however, has created the resemblance
most between the modern book and the old, is a
certain subconscious similarity in the authors,
strong enough, one supposes, to have ap-
proached the modern to the baroque even in
the case that he had never familiarized himself with the memoirs. Both are men of the
sort possessed by a sort of vanity which, while
moving them to lay hold upon the opportunity
of figuring in the brilliant world which their

birth and grace offers them, and of identifying
themselves with the radiance of great names
and pompous atmospheres, remains nevertheless too great, and too passive both, to make of
them the submissive courtiers. The pride of
Saint-Simon in an age of insane prides was
greater even than Louis'. He was out of grace
with the King for his resentment against the
encroachments of royalty on the privilege of
dukes; royalty felt the terrible passive proud-
ness, and bestowed its favors on less trucu-
lent subjects. But Saint-Simon too passion-
ately loved the order and ceremonial of the
court to accept exile. So he made good the
neglect to which his frail, nervous, irascible
temperament condemned him by sitting down
and carefully and unaffectedly recording
all the acts and ceremonies of the court of
which he was not one of the great suns; of ex-
amining the mechanism by which favorites
rose and privileges were gained; of setting
down the psychology of princes, ministers and
generals, and their odious habits; of recording
how it was that the King received the Duc de
Lorraine, and how the Spanish ambassador
saluted the young Philip V., and who it was
had the privilege of a *tabouret de grace* at

the court function, and why the education of the Duc de Bourgogne would have made him the most decent and bigoted of kings had not smallpox or influenza spared the state of France.

Somewhat the same situation was created by birth and temperament for Proust. Born on the lower slopes of society, full of desire to sun himself on the summits and thus compensate himself for the sense of insecurity with which his doubtful position and his over-sensitive temper filled him, loving beautiful manners and the poise of grand people as only refined souls can love them, it was predestined that he should both perceive the names Rohan and Montmorency, Richelieu and Foix—or whatever the originals of Guermantes and Bréaute, Marsantes and Chatellherault are— suffused with heraldic orange and purple and gold, and still always be something more than a charming snob. For if it was, of course, that Proust should love *les gens du monde,* and observe with delight the maneuvers of a society which had lost all its privileges, and still by some mysterious force maintained itself the cynosure of eyes and goal of myriad, virtuous, republican hearts, it was also of course that he should not remain on his knees another Henry James all his life, but perceive the hardness and the vulgarity of duchesses and highnesses and members of the Jockey Club. As in Saint-Simon, there was present here a pride as great as the greatest; and that pride would not accept as divine the order of even the most historical of societies, and found itself always measuring the faubourg against some conception of his own of what descent and aristocracy should be. So, both fascinated and critical at once, he became the best of memorialists of a little, enclosed and curious plane of life.

Of the qualities which charm in the novel of Marcel Proust, this light, telling painting of a singular and moribund little world will doubtless remain the most durable. The work will have an abiding interest as the record of a complex, hyper-sensitive, orchid-like sensibility. Besides, not Balzac has given more perfectly the poetry of snobbery, the intoxication and disillusionment of climbing. And still, the first of the qualities will surely prove the most resistant to wind and weather. There are certain books to which men go for a special sort of evocation. Saint-Simon's memoirs are one of these. The memoirs of Casanova, of a very different flavor, form another; for no one quite knows the sporty life of the eighteenth century who has not wandered about in them. And will not *A la recherche du temps perdu* eventually form another of this special series of books which deform a reality and create in its place a superior one? Here, too, there is a little tight cosmos into which one can creep. Proust has not the grand freshness and nobility of manner that was Saint-Simon's; nor the gorgeous sanguineness of the self-styled Chevalier de Seingault; he remains always the neurasthenic. But he has to tell with gusto and exquisite penetration of how it was the spiritual Duchess de Guermantes entertained her guests at dinner; of the salon of the slightly declassée Marquise where the noble faubourg and the intellectuals met; of the manners and mentalities of the leaders of fashion, the French friends of the Prince of Wales; of how Madame de Villeparisis cut M. Bloch at the time of the Dreyfus case; of the language and the unconscious self-revelations of M. de Charlus; of the young aristocratic girls of the dawning nineteenth century; of the evenings at the Princesse de Parma's; of the efforts of a for-

mer cocotte to climb into society; of the authors
and painters and actresses who were at various
times the protégés and the mistresses of the
circle of society women and clubmen. He has
to show a gallery of portraits of masters and
lacqueys, swells and cocottes, of all sorts of
people who figured in society in the nineties,
which stands almost Balzacian in its largeness
of conception and brilliance of detail. And
while there are born men of the world and
students of human nature and people curious
of aristocratic groups with traditions and
names and singular manners, he will remain
the hierophant of charming mysteries.

ALFRED KREYMBORG

ALFRED KREYMBORG

WALTER CONRAD ARENSBERG wished the motto of the first *Others* anthology to read: "The old expressions are with us always, but there are always others." But Alfred Kreymborg changed the conjunctive, and set the last clause running: "*and* there are always others"; thus early demonstrating his relationship to the poetic forms of the past. There never was, not even in the first hour of self-assertion, when his own subtle, acidulous and coquettish note seemed most strange and disequilibrating, any sentiment of conflict between the moderns and the classics in the mind of the poet of *Mushrooms*. The field of poetry for Kreymborg was no needle-point upon which one angel only might dance at a time; necessitating by its minuteness a state of rivalry, a movement of displacement and succession, between the older and the newer forms. The new day might summon a music tarter and more elusive than any which the past had seen emerge. Nevertheless, the

house of Phœbus had many chambers for this
new poet, and all examples of good song were
equally alive. All veritable lyric forms existed
beneficently side by side, affirming, illuminating, appreciating instead of warring on each
other's virtues. And the reverence for the
utterances of the great past men, and the established grandeurs of human life expressed in
the motto of *Others* and in the poetic hom-
ages to Bach and to Whitman, to Cézanne and
Schubert, was genuine in Kreymborg. It was
never to be questioned. Beside these possibly
deliberate expressions of comprehension of
values, there exists an undeliberate expression
perfectly capable of bearing forceful witness
to the fact that a living culture spread its
firmament deep above the rooves of Kreymborg's adobie huts. The crisp verbal minuets
precise in tempo, conceit, and metaphor and
cracklingly American; the poetry itself, demonstrates its presence.

Dainty, stiff and minuscule, *Mushrooms*
and *Blood of Things* positively affirm ultimate human values. Their matrix may lie in
the infantine state of being general in the community and usually productive of boastive and
rhetorical exhibition; enormous unnecessary

louds and fasts and larges: smears of soft;
brutalities and self-pitifulnesses. For Yankee
prudence and Yankee niggardliness with feeling have made it almost impossible for folk
this side the billow to plant the foot solidly
in an experience. The bosom finds itself in-
stinctively playing safe, and compensatory
acts in all mediums develop. But Kreymborg
remained perfectly faithful to the terms of
the miniature universal experience. He perceived the watery state of passion in himself
without application of any protective colora-
tion. Music and language, fancies and metaphors are homogeneous in his expressions and
true to his experience. No note is forced. The
music remains discreet, light, low, free of over-
emphasis, almost conversational in its reticence.
Its very key symbolizes matters small in scale
and not eternally serious; and balances exquisitely between pathos and humor, satire
and pity. The irreconcilable contradictions
of life are in it as neat little counterbobs and
balancement; the eternal dialogue of tiny head
and heart, of porcelain him and her. Manikin
and Minnikin, small positive infantine egos,
throw stony imperatives and categorical re-
fusals at one another inside measures that trip

and pirouet. Often, the music commences with
a sigh, holds a pleasant monotonousness with
lightly varied repetitions and slightest modula-
tions of tone, and dies away gradually in
strings of eddying subordinate clauses. Satire
tweaks a string or two in a corner of the brain,
then pauses innocently and mischievously.
The very words, polysyllabic though many of
them are, achieve an entirely laconic and
monosyllabic effect, stand separate and clipped
as nouns in a child's talk. It is a very large
child which speaks.

And the metaphors which cover the music,
metaphors extended in the case of the play-
lets to include scenery and the gestures of tight
frightened girls and blundering wistful boys
as well as the lyrics themselves, re-enforce the
picture. It is through articles and beings common to the ordinary round of days, the common city ways and sites that the poet perceives
the tragi-comedy of the insecure life he knows:
small cheap humble objects set suddenly for a
godlike instant aglow with high or humorous
significance. Love comes a ragpicker. One's
proper formula, elusive in the half-blind regions of the brain, is a fickle, summer-night
moth. Little ego, soaring above the earth in

ecstasy of self-love and playing with worlds, is a child tossing colored balloons. Poor harassed hens cackle; and one smiles and weeps over the loud feminists. The title of a group of poems, *The Round of a Five and Ten Cent Store,* might stand above all of them, so usual is it for Kreymborg to feel himself through small replicas, "seconds" many of them, nevertheless able to support life and contribute to its capital. *Blood of Things* contains a charming bestiary; but the animals treated therein might, with the exception of the camel, house in coops in a back yard; being parrakeets, owls, worms, robins, ducks, roaches, and hens. The beasts of prey and of large flight have not interested him.

It is almost impossible for an artist to find perfect fitness of expression if he have not a background of culture to help him render precise his feelings; and the exquisite justness of Kreymborg's representations, therefore, supplies indirect proof that the past was animate and the values always real for him. But one does not have to analyze the poet to establish the presence of feeling for the past. Assurance of it comes to one directly from out the poems. These little forms, strange-colored as upstart fungi, and not less American than Walt Whitman in all their subtlety, indirectness, irony, do indeed make life move outward. All feelings are interfitting, holding passkeys to one another; and the small pieces of Kreymborg, their size notwithstanding, bring one into relation with the grandeurs of human living. Wisdom, insight, a certain capacity for viewing his own experience objectively, permitted Kreymborg to keep the expression of his feelings proportionate. Even while he was laying his little eggs on the piano of the Liberal Club and waiting for the female to come along and fertilize them, the poet felt the largeness of life. And the truthfulness to scale constantly refers one to the human immensities against which the feelings, experiences, are thrown. The exact representations of the little heart's surges toward life, its contradictions and basenesses, the sharp satirization of the American pandemonium, therefore give us the reality and also the dream. We see, we reject, and are pointed once again sunward. Kreymborg may go among the great men a boy in short pants blowing a wooden whistle. But he keeps, through all his little rounds and ritournelles and satiric tootings, the rhythm of their mighty march.

Hence, when Kreymborg came to write the sonnets published in *Less Lonely,* his new volume, he moved with perfect logicality. He was attacking a form long felt and understood by him, and now brought into immediate relationship with him by his development. Some material more rebellious than his "free forms" was become necessary to him. Not alone Italy and the sense of solidity, of weight, of durable marble and bronze which is brought inevitably by the Mediterranean, had caused the graduation from perpetual kindergarten of America. Some interior sense of muscularity seems to have arrived. The poet, it would appear, had found himself not only among the classic cypresses and hills of Rome and of Maggiore; but farther, even in the broken world of afterwar, along the road which leads to the place of great living where male motives and agonies are. The poems, sonnets and free forms alike, are full of images of struggling revolting resistant objects: men who believe and sparks which "lead on again the universe"; and lyric with proud thanks and pity for them. Added to Kreymborg's native subtlety, wit, and charm; fused with his capricious dourness of fancy, and his concision and obliquity of statement, there spreads itself a new and almost oriental voluptuousness of color. Even in *Blood of Things* there is no piece as rich as *And White the White Invokes*. But not alone the sonnets and poems in blank verse in *Less Lonely* exhibit new sonority and largeness of flow. The pieces resembling the old "free forms": little rondos and twinkling metric figures unrhymed or only very lightly rhymed; *Italian Stream, Peasant, Dawn, Pushcart, Adagio,* show a new firmness of line. Kreymborg is no longer shy of direct expression. Full of this new certainty, then, it was inevitable that this poet of intimacies should try himself out against the intimate resistant form of the sonnet.

He has been astonishingly agile with the "small key" of Petrarch and of Shakespeare. To be sure, the mold has occasionally defeated him. The five sonnets on *Savonarola Burning* are a little coldly noble and impersonal. In other sonnets, less rhetorical and more pungent, the inspiration flags momentarily and the hand laboriously stuffs the holes.

Sometimes the thought becomes mortally congested in the form. But none are entirely without some fine brushing of gray, some happy conceit or turn of phrase, some fine wistfulness or largeness of thought; and seven or eight, among them *The Mountains Stoop to Hills, Quite High Enough or Low, A Ribbon Two Yards Wide, When They Require Gardens* and *Another Grieving Forest* ring new and round, and bring Kreymborg's fine simplicity again. It is reassuring to find him developing his small but nevertheless authentic *maestria;* and in a time when so many promising literary edifices stand like incompleted houses raised no farther than the ground floor, to hear him hammering steadily on the second story of his own.

WALLACE STEVENS

WALLACE STEVENS

THE playing of a Chinese orchestra. On a gong a bonze creates a copper din. The most amazing cacophany amid dissolving labials and silkiest sibilants. Quirks, booms, whistles, quavers. Lord, what instruments has he there? Small muffled drums? Plucked wires? The falsetto of an ecstatic eunuch? Upon deliberate examination it appears Stevens' matter is the perfectly grammatical arrangement of an English vocabulary not too abstract, Elizabethan, legal, with accidentals of alien terms and purely imitative sounds. But so novel and fantastic is the tintinnabulation of unusual words, and words unusually rhythmed and arranged, that you nearly overlook the significations, and hear outlandish sharp and melting musics. While the motley collection prances past, a horn winds its golden cantilene; funeral tam-tams pulse; a violin modulates sharply through quarter-tones and metal particles chunk and chink. Irregular and occasional interior rhymes furnish curious accords. And

mixed with the instrumental tones, the fowl
persuasion utters its proper squawky staccato:
clucking of strutting bantams—

> "Chieftain Iffucan of Azcan in caftan
> Of tan with henna hackles, halt!'';

parleyings of cockatoos in tropic woods—

> "He is not paradise of parakeets
> Of his gold ether, golden alguazil.''

Together with new auditory sensations, the
poems of Wallace Stevens release new intensities of visual ones. Music remains the prime
element of this diverting art; with Alfred
Kreymborg the author represents the musical
imagist; nevertheless he lets us perceive sea-
water

> "dissolved in shifting diaphanes
> Of blue and green,''

as well as hear it swish 'longside the boat; and
brings with the whisper of the surf upon
Florida beaches the nuances of balmy summer
twilights. And the visual imagery alternates
extremely refined with biting forceful impressions no less suavely and deliciously than does
the auditory. Stevens is precise among the

shyest, most elusive of movements and shad-
ings. He sees distinctly by way of delicacy the
undulations of the pigeon sinking downward,
the darkening of a calm among water-lights,
the variations of the deep-blue tones in dusky
landscapes. Quite as regularly as the colors
themselves, it is their shades of difference that
are registered by him:

> "green sides
> And gold sides of green sides";

> "raspberry tanagers in palms
> High up in orange air";

> "sea-shades and sky-shades
> Like umbrellas in Java";

Yet this fastidious, aristocratic nature possesses a blunt power of utterance, a concen-
trated violence, that is almost naturalistic.
Stevens recognizes the cruel, the combative
principles of life as well as the soft and yield-
ing; sees hanging by the side of the "golden
gourds" he loves to contemplate, some "warty
squashes, streaked and rayed"; knows that together with purple tufts and scarlet crowns
the tropics hold "the green vine angering for
life." We discover him momentarily piling
gristling images, fine roughnesses of color and

acrid turns of language upon each other, hacking with lines of poetry and banging harsh rhyme upon rhyme. *Last Looks at the Lilacs* and *Floral Decorations for Bananas,* for all their levity of manner, approach the pitch of crude and ferocious language.

But sensation alone is liberated to new intensities by Stevens' forms. Emotion, on the contrary, is curiously constrained by them within a small range of experience and small volumes of expression. The title *Harmonium,* given by the author to his unique collection, makes to declare this littleness the effect entirely of deliberate simplification, and the conscious accommodation of matter to the range of an intimate instrument. But *Harmonium* seems to us something of a misnomer. Stevens appears to us not so much with the aspect of the austere artist as with that of the artist mysteriously, disconcertingly faithful to the technique of an instrument long transcended by the requirements of his nature and incapable of drawing out of himself in all their power his latent emotions. He resembles one born, say, for the grand piano who, while lovingly touching the keys as only the born pianist can, nevertheless persists in using certain processes appropriate to the reed-organ, and consequently produces a strange and hybrid music, half Strawinsky and half hymn-tune. That chamber-orchestra of his, with its range of novel and delightful sounds—he has a genuine feeling for it. He loves its odd and piercing timbres, and toys bewitchingly with them. And still, we get no indication of its real limits. We are never given to know quite the fulness of its dynamics; it is too exclusively engaged in *chinoiseries*. Stevens' rhythms are chiefly secondary rhythms. Scarcely ever is his attack a direct and simple one. Generally, it is oblique, patronizing and twisted with self-intended mockery. The measure is sometimes languid, sometimes mincing, almost invariably buffoon-like. It trips, pirouettes, executes an hundred little foppish turns and graces. It rocks complacently like a preening water-fowl upon its perch; waltzes in grotesque fury; keens like a comic rabbi; begins a movement and lets it end in air. Besides, the humor is consistently personal in reference. The poet is perceived leaning in evident boredom against the corner of a mantlepiece, or adjusting his monocle with a look of martyrdom.

Another Pierrot. The white clown will not

from the pages. For as defined by Laforgue
and his following he stands the spiritual type
of all correct young men in mourning, like
Wallace Stevens, for an "I-the-Magnificent."
You recalled it was too evident Destiny intended that Lord Pierrot play a princely
tragic rôle. She gave him noble melancholy,
contempt for the vulgar, proud port and
gesture; poured into his mold the very
stuff of Hamlets. Unfortunately, Pierrot
glanced down along his body; and as he
did so, it seemed to him that he was clad in
loose flopping ridiculous raiment. And the
sentiment of the preposterousness of his person follows the white clown more faithfully
than a shadow, and lays fingers of ice
on every living moment. Uncomfortably
self-aware, the pitiable gentleman can
never quite spend himself in living, and
remains emotionally naïve, O Horrors! as
a romantic poet. To be sure, little in his
mask betrays him. Pierrot is sophisticated,
worldly, lettered, read in philosophical authors Greek and Germanic. He is excessively
correct, partly from natural elegance and
partly in protest against romantic dishevel-
ment; and functions suavely as reader to an

empress, teller of a London bank, or lawyer in Hartford, Connecticut. Nevertheless, his unprojected energies and nobilities and grandiosities are perpetually assuming shapes of self-pity, yearning for enveloping love, and woman-worship; and although Pierrot is entirely too aware to mistake them for cosmic pains or enchantments of the heart, his sentimentalities threaten shamelessly to overcome him, and add immeasurably to his embarrassment. Hence his ideal self, the cruelly murdered "I-the-Magnificent," incapable of revealing itself in all its princeliness, gains satisfaction in the shape of revenge. It takes the exaltations of the subject emotional self, and very archly turns them into parody. Of melancholy soliloquy and philosophical dudgeon it makes a silvery music signifying nothing. Amid the tinkling ice of exquisite perceptions it lightly ridicules the objects of sentimental effusion, diverts the emotional current toward slightly grotesque ones, or comes

> "as belle design
> Of foppish line";

thus simultaneously ceding to the pressure of

inferior emotion and attesting amid extravagant waltzes and verbal fireworks its own ineffable superiorities.

Nor is Wallace Stevens the sole distinguished American poet of distinct Laforguian cut. Lord Pierrot is called T. S. Eliot, too, and sports other and smaller names as well. The series is a perfectly natural one. American life has hitherto tended to excite the painful tension between the two portions of the self, so determining a factor in the Laforguian expression; the curiously Yankee flavor of the parodistic manner of the "Watteau of the café-concerts," and of his ironic usage of journalistic and demotic idiom, has been remarked by not a few critics. Certainly, each of the new western additions to the company, poorer in general virtuosity than their great architype although they are, have enriched the tradition with a perfectly individual color, and enlarged its scope. Stevens, for example, is full of a jazzy American sensuousness; and the polyglot American towns have made him peculiarly sensitive to the unusual and remote sounds of the English language. Nevertheless, the expression which he brings amid flowers, frost and "good fat guzzly fruit," remains to

a degree characteristic of the school. His
music is a music signaled as vain, an exaltation not so much "without sound" as without
object, a bland, curiously philosophical movement of the soul without signification. What
he has to say appears too useless for him to
say it out. The words, deliciously Elizabethan
and comically abstract, remain "musical"
merely, morsels rolled upon an epicure's palate. And world-weariness becomes an *Invective
against Swans,* woman-worship a burlesque
hymn to *Heavenly Vincentine,* and exaltation
takes idly to tracing the processional of clouds
across the sky. The senses dance, but they
achieve only a sort of titillation, a vague
naughtiness; intelligence sits coldly in the
center of the ring and directs their gyrations.
The disillusionments troop across: the story
of the wildcat which always bars the center
of the road and falls asleep only in death;
Florida nights which yield nothing more than
a caress of finger-tips; love turned stale at
forty; vain dreams erected "upon the basis
of the common drudge." The lengthy narrative poem *The Comedian as the Letter C*
contains the history of a poetic career, the
feeling of the war, the hope of a national ex-

pression, the tragedy of environment; but it secretes them behind a shimmer of language and archness piled upon archness; and takes for its protagonist—Crispin.

In spite of its perfect things, "Nuances of a Theme of Williams" and the others, *Harmonium* does not, therefore, entirely represent the day. Little reveals the movement which has occurred in the American mind of late more simply than the fact that we should willingly feel its qualities of evasiveness, of archness and comic pudicity as slightly timed. The characteristic note of 1890 was not outworn for us ten years ago; and yet, to-day, even though nothing in the basic character of life appears transformed, and Plymouth Rock in the bosom of all has not offered to melt, or freemen's arms grown lighter, we have transcended it. We are somewhat less self-aware; and irritated by what tends to recall us to the old bad consciousness. And it is precisely embarrassment, shyness and holy shame which do the wicked work; we find the attitude of the Venus de' Medici suggestive. An impulse in us bids authors be more simple and direct, and give completely what they feel; above all to advance from behind the curtain of language.

Tragical disabilities are the very ordinary stuff of life, and what to-day requires most is impersonality, perspective, objectivity. No need subtracting from James Joyce.—And yet, *Harmonium* remains one of the jewel-boxes of contemporary verse. If certain of its elements appear a trifle outworn, others very definitely thrust the art of poetry toward unknown boundaries. As a musician, Stevens is revealed an almost impeccable craftsman. Not only is his idiom new and delicious; his surface is almost invariably complete. Experimental rhymes have an inevitability under his hands, and his rhythms do not break. He produces his material as conceived by him with exquisite tact, giving the just amount, and not recovering traversed ground. The terminations and cadences of his pieces are usually quite unpredictable; only very rarely, as in *Six Significant Landscapes,* do the final surprising extensions of the idea grow mechanical. We have a number of artists working in the medium of poetry; Pound, Eliot and others have produced work both delicate and hard. Yet the arrival of a volume of verse on each of its one hundred and twenty odd pages very patently the pretty booklet *arida modo pumice expolitum* is an event not hitherto seen by our generation. And for the moment Wallace Stevens remains eminently the artist in his field.

MARIANNE MOORE

MARIANNE MOORE

NEVER have exquisite perceptions appeared so loosely set. Sensations of the curious pungency of

> "a walnut rind
> Of oak-leaves and plucked mullein on the brae";

delicately evocative phrases—

> "The learned scenery of Egypt";

> "England
> with its baby rivers and little towns";

> "It is a far cry from 'the queen full of jewels'
> And the beau with the muff
> From the gilt coach shaped like a perfume bottle
> To the conjunction of the Monongahela and the
> Allegheny"

resemble at first sight brilliants hung to a string or assembled pell-mell in a sack. We miss a unifying pitch or music, and Whitman looms mightily formal and sustained. The poems, each with its carefully synthesized vocabulary, recall rambling parenthetical discourses; gradually only does the graphite turn into diamond. Yet finally the whimsical essays are seen substances dense and winged as the elder poetry. There is distinctly a form, a surface, a music. "The jade and the rock-crystal course about in solution." It is evident Marianne Moore has dissolved the materials of her art and re-formed them about an original principle.

This principle is a noble relaxedness and calmness of movement. She draws her breath in light serenity and equipoise. There is in her a balance so old-fashioned, "so old-fashionable," that it is in process of becoming interesting to us again. Although like Hebrew poetry her work may be called "prose with a heightened consciousness," since "ecstasy affords the occasion and expediency determines the form," it remains singularly free of the respiration of Bayreuth and almost religiously quiet; and it is precisely this replacement of exaltation by genteel evenness of tone and slow uncoiling that baffles us so, unused as we are to finding poets without some trace of poetic "rapture." Yet she is always moved, and her feeling is intense. Sadness hovers over ever so many of her moods, and seems never en-

tirely removed from any of them, even the
lightest and briskest, sparkling satire. She can
be strong and emphatic: climaxes of emotion
widen her utterances to statements that are
like banners planted and rocks affirmed. Only,
the melancholy and the laughter, the biblical
prophecy and finest tinglings of the nerves lie
all of them upon a line that makes no violent
deflections, inscribes no gulf-like curves, and
sustains itself amid its convolutions upon its
own cool, aristocratic, "normal" level. If any
verse affords the "quiet breathing," it is
Marianne Moore's. We had no idea that such
light, racy and silvery touches, such delicate
joints and sound of low swishing waves could
prove as rich and powerful, and the economy
works as an enchantment.

They are established, those nobly easy movements and tranquil tones, it seems by the lei-
surely and intricate fashion in which the poet's
ideas unroll themselves from the ball of experience. She has a golden, excessively subtle
and ingenious wit: the chief ingredient, keen-
ness of perception, is very strongly developed
in her. Witness, the pungent oblique sensations, unconsciously feminine in every trait,
which she has managed to capture—

"... The water drives a wedge
    of iron through the edge
of the cliff, whereupon the stars
pink
rice-grains, ink
    bespattered jelly-fish, crabs like
    green
    lilies and submarine
toadstools, slide each on the other,"

or

"raw silk—ivory white, snow white,
oyster white and six others—"

The ingredient of intuition is likewise very awakened in her; give her but "the end of a golden string," a few bits of furniture, a fragment of stuff, and she will pinch them with the clever fingers of the psychic, and delicately infer from textures, shapes and lines, lives of people, periods and landscapes. And few living writers possess a riper sense of racy, unpretentious aptnesses of expression. Her own word-structures, it has been seen, have epigrammatic magnificence; one seems to hear the chisel carving a Latin inscription in stone, they ring so lapidary. Her work gives edge and fulness of value to innumerable American stereotypes; and incrustated in its surface one finds pithy, gamy, unprecious expressions culled by her in the course of her most ad-

venturous reading, for she is a very scholarly
poet; and quoted in enthusiasm for niceness.
Hence, her amazing wit; the perceptivity, and
feeling for aptness of expression having very
naturally developed into an ingenuity in the
perception and expression of the connection
between ideas, and in the unification of ideas
possessing resemblance and congruity. And
consequently the form of her lyricism. Some
homely familiar object, a steam-roller, a cat
"taking its prey to privacy," a woman's dress
and manner, a glimpse and whiff of the port
of New York, is suddenly seen a manner of
shorthand account of an intangible inner thing,
personal or social, a prelude to adventure,
a picture of man's rapacity trumped by
death's. The relationship existing between the
various material traits adumbrates those existing between the spiritual. Or, as in the poem
Marriage, a number of images and phrases will
suddenly refer her to a superficially simple
thing, and immeasurably increase its significance and illuminate its comedy. And then the
swift perceptions and acute expressions of
these connections and relationships stream
forth in close subtle order, dovetailing with
each other at the most astonishing angles, in-

terrupting each other, dissolving swiftly one into the other. For her mind, the proximities between these apparently unrelated ideas are very intense; and so she sees, clenches, and then is through long before others see, clench and begin to absorb; and so she seems perpetually interrupting herself, and breaking her thought off when indeed she is merely progressing directly on her way. She is an inventor of rapid transits, swift of process as Beethoven in his last sonatas and quartets. If she is cryptic at times, it is not wilful at all, but from the blood: the American is a cryptic speaker; crypticism is almost the genius of his literature. Till at length the secret accompanist of mental alacrity, secret cause and end of it appears in full, the easy movement, the relaxed rhythm, the quiet "normal" way of breathing; and the poem exists out in the world.

Not that it invariably succeeds in establishing itself entire. Occasionally the poet fails to bring her gliding currents and lightly mounting waves to the perfect rest or summit. There may of course reside some finality in phrases such as those which conclude *Dock Rats* and *Poetry:*

". . . to one who has been accustomed to it, shipping is
  the most congenial thing in the world,"

and

". . . that which is, on the other hand,
  genuine then you are interested in poetry";

nevertheless to us their prosiness arrests the
movement, and indicates that the conclusion
was achieved by force of will alone. But such
recalcitrancies are rare in her. *The Fish*
moves throughout with a smooth watery
glide. *Black Earth* unfolds itself like a heraldic pennant in the breeze. In *Graveyard*
Miss Moore has given a dense solid symphony
majestic of movement and low of climax, perfectly sustained in its quiet tone, and pleas-
antly dour in color; this noble poem and certain
of her most recent things, *Marriage, Octopus*
and *People's Surroundings,* constitute "something durable like the art of the museums."

We have no classes in America; universal
dulness covers all. Yet though we have no
classes, and masses only, we begin again to
possess a small minority desiring quality in
people and in things. It is from out this group
that the public of Marianne Moore will constitute itself. Aristocracy of being remains so

much a thing of standing walls, of feeling and
of thinking prompt, fine and intolerant of sentimentality; and her walls are always up,
crowned with laughter and clear vision. We
see a slender tower looking out over the open
sea, and the sea wears a sinister aspect; and the
vulgarity of America, its insensibility, easi-
ness, materialism, league about by land. Miss
Moore feels the weights borne in upon her
ramparts, threatening the temper of her
mind; many of her poems reveal wounds
wrought by what she finds people doing round
about her. Yet so steadfast is her craving for
quality and her allegiance to the thing she
deeply is, that the walls resist the pressure, the
Greek fire plays, the standard floats. Balanced
sensibility and edge maintain themselves; common objects and common expressions come to
contain in themselves more and more of the
inner life. Thus her poems become "a pun-
gence which strengthens the nerves of the
brain" in others. That is not their primary
objective, certainly. Miss Moore is wholly lost
in her ideas, tragic glances seaward, noble pro-
tests, philosophical visions of ordinary circumstances. It is these she intends bringing, in
their forms of slow hissing music, and in all

passion of workmanship. She is a genuinely objective poet. But precisely for this reason will her work be felt the summons and high stay to quality.

MARSDEN HARTLEY

MARSDEN HARTLEY

HARTLEY is an artist born like Whistler and like Blake not to a single medium alone. Color remains the major medium of this expressionistic New Englander, and confidant of his larger moods; but the distinguishedness, the airy apartness which glints from every canvas and every plate of glass rubbed by the painter informs also his pieces of poetry and his prose. He stands among the most rare, fanciful and dainty of living essayists. To literature he brings a naturally beauteous flow of language, a very poet's flow gushing spontaneously out from him in easy richness, and depositing a magnificence of substance lightly cadenced. Stemming as a prose-man one would say from Walter Pater, Francis Thompson and Henry James, fellow Parnassians; painting the lily, stroking satins, silks and velvets, and hammering much precious gold, he has interspersed the ceremonial slow gestures of his forebears with lighter, more conversational, less priestly ones; and made of their opulent verbal matter a racier, fluffier and more frivolous thing. The pomp of heavily ritualistic cults remains in his blood; but for the moment it is veiled by the dandy's affectedly careless conduct of gloves and swaggerstick, and sit of tile and gardenia. Perceptions of beauty and iridescent fancies are modulated to the tone of superior spiritual talk; made portion of an esthetic of ordinary living seriously developed by a spirit exquisitely temperate and urbane. Doubtless the author would be pleased to give his readers the sensation of participating with him in the happiest, most inspired of informal conversations; of having met him promenading on Fifth Avenue in the fair humor produced say by the news that he had been elected corresponding member of the international society of dadas; and strolling with him, visiting a gallery or two, taking in a turn at a vaudeville house, stepping into a circus dressing room for a moment while commenting epigrammatically on Cézanne and acrobatics, the poetry of the nineties and photography, May Wirth the equestrienne and Georgia O'Keeffe. Frankly he announces

"I like tea chit-chat. Words are never meant to
mean anything then. They are simply given
legs and wings and they jump and fly. They
land where they can, and fall flat if they must."

And with deliberate purpose he cultivates a
well-bred ease in Zion.

The subject-matter which has excited this
precious and racy flow of language extends,
in accordance with the writer's own rhythm,
beyond the limits usually assigned to esthetic
meditation. Hartley discourses upon Ryder
and the buffalo dance of the Tesuque pueblo,
on Stieglitz and New England precieux and
the poetry of Ernest Dowson; but he dwells
with equal delight upon jolly and curious fragments of unthinking life, "minstrels of mus-
cular melody," tumblers and trapeze swingers
and circus clowns, and on some vaudeville girls
who play ivory and silver diamond-studded
accordions. *Adventures in the Arts* is made
up part of essays on modern painting, part of
essays on poets, Thompson, Emily Dickinson,
Dowson and Adelaide Crapsey, and part of
pieces significantly entitled *The Twilight of
the Acrobat, Vaudeville,* and *A Charming
Equestrienne.* Not that this informality
is out of style. On the contrary, it is a legiti-

mate extension of the Parnassian interest; before Hartley, Arthur Symons reconciled an' interest in Verlaine and in the music-hall, and played with the charming levities of Dieppe. The Parnassian's excitant is the physical splendor of the world. Humbler and quotidian stuffs, the homely subjects which serve the great affirmers of life, Rembrandt and Whitman and Moussorgsky, he passes; uninspired by them. Give him material brave of surface, and he waxes incandescent as his freer companions. And it is precisely because he finds in acrobats a physical magnificence like to the magnificences of works of art, that Hartley matches paint with circuses. Handsome color and animal grace are his criteria:

"The men and women of vaudeville transform themselves into lovely flowers and animal forms; and the animals take on semblances of human sensibility in vaudeville. It is the superb arabesque of the beautiful human body that I care for most, and get the most from in those cameolike bits of beauty and of art. So brief are they, and like the wonders of sea gardens as you look through the glass bottoms of the little boats. So like the wonders of the microscope, full of surprising novelties of color and form. So like the kaleidoscope in the ever changing, ever shifting bits of color reflecting each other, falling into new patterns with each twist of the toy. If you care for the iridescence of the moment you

will trust vaudeville as you are not able to
trust any other sort of performance. You
have no chance for the fatigue of the problem.
You are at rest as far as thinking is concerned.
It is something for the eye first and last.—For
me, they (the vaudevillians) are the saviours
for the dullest art in existence, the art of the
stage. The stage is not the place for imitation
and photography. It is a place for the laughter
of the senses, for the laughter of the body. It
is a place for the tumbling blocks of the brain
to fall in heaps.''

So Hartley's book of prose lays claim to the
shelf upon which Pater and Arthur Symons
stand; beneath the surface of the playfulness
there shines a receptivity to beauty kin to
theirs. Whether he writes of a vaudeville
gymnast who ''gives you chiefly the impres-
sion of a dragon-fly blown in the wind of a
brisk morning over cool stretches of water.
You would expect him to land on a lily-pad
any moment and smooth his wings with his
needle-like legs''; or of Odilon Redon ''wor-
shiper of the lip of the flower, of dust upon
the moth wing, of the throat of the young girl
or the brow of the young boy,'' he transmits
impulsions freshly pricked from life. In some
remote fashion Hartley is the lover of these
circus-people, little equestriennes and birds of
the trapeze heavens and Irene Franklin and

Ella Shields and "that other great woman," Fay Templeton; just as he is the lover of Adelaide Crapsey and Emily Dickinson and "some women artists." Hence, when he comes to write of his own brothers, he knows the England of the artist-mind better than those "who only England know." He is a poet in criticism, a developed, often brilliant, always sensitive personality mobilized for the definition of quality, translating into life again through literature the sensations received from the work of his forerunners and contemporaries. Either too indifferent or too subtle, one scarcely knows which, to estheticize, he scarcely ever fails of seizing upon the quality of life communicated by the work of the painters with which he has lived, the substance without sense of which all technical analysis is vain, and of incarnating it automatically in a crisp verbal image, or passage of appropriately tinted prose.

One must go to *Adventures in the Arts* for the justest, warmest, most poetical vision of the ritual dances of the American Indians. Hartley has seen these fluid works of art with brilliant perceptivity. He has felt their religious origin in himself. And his description

of the work of these great artists became of
itself a supplication for the artist in America
submitted to the trampling, uncultured crowd
of whites. And one must go to him for some
of the daintiest papers on American painting
which have been written, those contributed by
Willard Huntington Wright to "The Forum"
not excepted; for deep understanding and exact appraisement of Ryder, Homer, Twacht-
man, Fuller, Robinson, Martin, Marin,
O'Keeffe and poor Rex Slinkard. You could
scrutinize a long while the color-language of
Ryder without arriving at any verbal picture
more sympathetic than Hartley's:

"There is quiet, solace, if you will, in Michel, in
Courbet, but there is never a rest for the eye or
the mind or the spirit in those most awesome of
pictures which Ryder has presented to us, few
as they are; for the Ryder legend is akin to the
legend of Giorgione. There is always splendor
in them but it is the splendor of the dream given
over to a genius more powerful than the vision
which has conjured them forth. It is distinctly
a land of Luthany in which they have their being; he has inscribed for us that utter home-
lessness of the spirit in the far tracts that exist
in the realm of the imagination; there is suffering in his pictures, that fainting of the spirit
that breathlessness which overtakes the soul in
search of the consummation of beauty."

He paints an O'Keeffe in writing of the work of this young woman:

> "With Georgia O'Keeffe one takes a far jump into volcanic crateral ethers, and sees the world of woman turned inside out and gaping with deep open eyes and fixed mouth at the rather trivial world of living people.—Georgia O'Keeffe has had her feet scorched in the laval effusiveness of terrible experience; she has walked on fire and listened to the hissing of vapors round her person. The pictures of O'Keeffe are probably as living and shameless private documents as exist, in painting certainly and probably in any other art. By shamelessness I mean unqualified nakedness of statement. She is far nearer to St. Theresa's version of life as experience than she could ever be to that of Catherine the Great or Lucrezia Borgia. Georgia O'Keeffe wears no poisoned emeralds. She wears too much white; she is impaled with a white consciousness."

Indeed, there are perhaps only two distinct overvaluations in the book: one of Dodge Macknight and one of Arthur B. Davies. Of the latter, Hartley writes:

> "He is the highly sensitized illustrator appointed by the states of his soul to picture forth the pauses of the journey through the realm of fancy. It has in it the passion of violet and silver dreaming, the hue of an endless dawn before the day descends upon the world. You expect the lute to regain its jaded tune there. You expect the harp to reverberate once again with the old fervors. You expect the syrinx to

unfold the story of the reed in light song. It
contains the history of all the hushed horizons
that can be found over the edges of a world of
materiality. It holds in it always the warm
soul of every digit of the moon.''

To be able to write in this fashion, one must
believe a little unreservedly that men are to be
judged exclusively by what they intend and not
by what they achieve.

Like the more imaginative passages of his
prose, much of Hartley's coldly splendid
poetry consists, in the light movement of
the magnificent phrases which seem to come to
him with so much happy readiness. Certain
of the poems, ''The Crucifixion of Noel'' and
''Blue Fruit'' in particular, appear deliberately decorative in effect; reliquaries of
precious phrases and images assembled about
a certain key, that of blue especially; and
Hartley has proven himself adept in this decorative and essentially limited use of language. But there are others which, still
characteristically incrustated with verbal
brilliants and conversational in tone, have content, express a lyrical mood, and make without any heaviness, a confession from the heart.
A man of the world speaks, without emphasis, and with dispassionate gesture; but to

the subtle he demonstrates lacerated flesh held together only by means of a carefully studied decorum. "Gulls at Gloucester" and "The Inquisition" have the superior unity begotten of feeling. And some of the macabre dramatic pieces, "Boston Portrait Projections" and other studies of the perverse New England temper, awake a peculiar shudder, a creepiness of attics and rats and suicidal ropes. This is "Spoon River" way down east; and not in Robinson or O'Neill has the wrongness of præcoxy men and manic women found a more appropriately elliptical, madly calm and rasping form.

Like painter, like author. If Hartley the proseman and the poet, whether he be discussing paint or circuses, or setting forth the sensations gotten on a trip up the Woolworth belfry, exhibits something of the same glimmer of genius which makes his pigment vibrate, Hartley the proseman and poet exhibits some of the same shortcomings which limit the effectiveness of the brushman. As a painter, some nervous instability perhaps prevents him developing many of his pictures into satisfactorily solid organisms. He seems oftentimes to break off and become wearied

too soon. Some noble distinction, some ingenious fancy he inevitably records; too seldom
the whole fine presence of the fully marshaled
interest. And holes and thinnesses yawn
throughout his essay-writing. The organization of the material is not always athletic. The
essay on Winslow Homer sprawls and circles
about itself; one would give much to have been
able to place it in the hands of some poor college prig for stiffening. Even as colored and
profound a piece of writing as the chapter on
the Red Man, with its subtle relation of Indian
ritual dancer and modern artist, wanders
slightly. Other of the studies annoy momentarily with bare unsupported statements. Too
often one is dismissed with an airy waving of
a hand. But it is useless to cry over the un-
spilled milk. Hartley the painter remains one
of the significant figures in the contemporary
situation in art; and Hartley the essayist is
one of the divining living critics. He is at all
times the man who works only when some perception is big in his brain and wants delivery.
Other men paint and write in order to have
money, or to have admiration, or to justify
themselves, or for the reason that inside them
some feeling of responsibility to the world or

some other personage drives them forward. But Hartley is delighted by the splendors of the world, and sufficiently civilized to entertain his own perceptions of things and set them forth. And it is precisely this unfailing chastity of the artist, this faithfulness to inner necessity, which gives his work in either medium its value, and places us so richly in his debt.

E. E. CUMMINGS

E. E. CUMMINGS

GREAT cleanness distinguishes *The Enormous Room*. With unswerving fidelity the eye of the author has followed his line of interest through the jumble of materials. The narrative sets forth a surprising utter illogicality. Cummings' world is a complex of startling turns and atrocicus sudden comic arrivals of the unforeseen. Events careen eccentrically from each other like blocks that refuse to fall end against end, and follow incomprehensible patterns. Unsuspected edges of flint lead 'round corners to equally unsuspected surfaces of silk, and queer little lovelinesses sprout from damp stones. Objects behave like monkey-men abrupt and ridiculous of movement, and men appear whirring mechanisms and terrible toys. The irregular rhythm of a clown-god is apparent: his majesty of unreason, the white moon himself, dizzily zigzagging through the universe and shedding in marvelous dislocation delight, brickbats and death.

Butt of a great white joke, Cummings observed with awe and fascination the perfectly unreasonable geometry of cosmic antics. A crowded room proved enormous, unlimited; the whole wide world was a prison; and a prison, freedom. The two American lads in the detention pen of La Ferté Macé, so differently grounded from the remainder of the poor prisoners and yet so wholly portion of the general life, were symbolical presences, it now appears. American imagination has not hitherto consented to dwell in the house of the living dead. Knowledge of helpless unprotected life, of dirt and sores and lowliness has been rejected, the subject externalized and sentimentalized. The Americans have not suffered and they have fled from suffering. Puritanism has made righteousness synonymous with an income of thirty-five thousand a year. Conscience of humiliation, failure and sorrow have been considered evidence of biological inferiority. Because of this vanity, America has not as yet begot her soul. But Cummings, like a European caught in the shambles, and with the grace of the born poet, underwent the experience to the utmost of his youthful capacity. When he and his friend

B—— were abducted by the French government from the Norton Harjes Ambulance outfit in which they were voluntarily serving, and entombed as seditious suspects in a miserable jail, a misfortune got converted into treasure. Sense of the magnificent illogicality of life and of the Chaplinade of the adventure erected itself; an universal situation was felt. The joke, the novelty, and the vivacity of sensations were too strong for the purely personal feelings; Cummings tells us with what disdain he and his friend refused the offer of privacy in the prison hospital against a bribe. Sympathy turned feelings of personal resentment into resentment of injustice in behalf of oppressed individuals; and sympathy discovered priceless fragments of the everpresent wonder of life lying about in the dustheap. Cummings himself has placed the sharp and delicious account of his captivity under the sign of *The Pilgrim's Progress,* and called chapters of it Apollyon and The Delectable Mountains; and what happened to him constituted indeed progress of the soul in a youthful pilgrim from New England. Braces against the whole of life broke down when this young poet accepted the dirt and let the truth have him entire. Hampering shame and loathing, and fear of things more universal than the muck, were overcome. It is noteworthy that the first chapters of *The Enormous Room* describe with the zest of a soul winning its freedom through contacts with ugly and painful realities of the sort withheld from protected people, while the later ones are drunkenly lyrical with rare human tenderness. The book stops on a note of wild proud affirmation of life and hope of men and women; through experience soul was come in truth into new territory.

A new, crisp, brindled style had presented itself for birth. The prose forming Cummings' vision of the illogical will of things and the unsuspected affinities between pain and delight, leads one out among advertising, skyscrapers and movies. The verbal integument affirms ultimate values, since it remains organic and subtle; and still it does not contradict the style of life existing in American streets and assembly places. Something of the quality of the popular forms circulates within its own dainty, gay and whimsical turns. It contains as principle the pleasant not unhealthy unripeness informing the hidden spirit of American life, the hardness of a growing object resisting premature decay. The rich German language has the word in *herb*. Or, it is a trifle like American ice-cream; for, as everyone knows, the difference between French ice-cream and American is that the one is made with certain warm, passionate elements left out of the composition of the other. And, shrilly pitched, caricatural even more in tempo than in tendency, taut of rhythm, Cummings' prose relates rebellious matters, never before associated, with exquisite smoothness of modulation. It juxtaposes ancient elegances and brutalities of expression, sensitively employed traditional idiom and gamiest crudities of the vernacular. Adverbs are permitted to qualify nouns. Words pour forth in forbidden order at the dictation of rhythm. Words are used purely for their overtones and their sensational impact in quick pencil-like delimitations of a person, a scene, a mood, a smell. In moments of intense excitement a verbal scandal explodes. Enormities of wit, metaphors abstracted from the studio and the street-corner span almost impossible widths in marking the dizzy rhythm and strange relationships of objects. A prison stinks and blossoms fantastically. Only momentarily, as in the scene at the wayside crucifix, does an excessive pudicity hold the expression below the intensity demanded by the situation; and only momentarily, as in the close of the chapter called *Jean le Nègre,* does it overshoot the goal and verge on sentimentality. A ferocious sarcasm is restrained, a piece of life held firm with objective hand. Cummings' narrative stands with *Opfergang* by Fritz von Unruh in the forefront of truly distinguished writings born of the war; and the American is perhaps the more creative. The German tale flows from out a culture of the heart deeper perhaps than Cummings'; the American nevertheless embodies the play of a marvelous sensuous instinct for prose, and lies a little further up the road of estheticism.

Again a many-stopped instrument has appeared for music. The poems fill out the picture started by the prose. Open *Tulips and Chimneys* at any page, and somewhere upon that page there will be traces, oftentimes thrilling ones, of an inner musical state playing exuberantly with the materials of life. The swift succession of crisp tactile sensations

and metaphors, the fastidious and delightful
array of words, entertain the fancy with the
idea that some goldsmith-painter of the
Renaissance has come to give a verbal equivalent for the arabesques, curls, and airy ripples
of Gozzoli and Ghirlandajo. The idiom makes
a direct response to life: Cummings'
"smears," his complexes of mutually resistant
words, his agglutinations, register elements
of the American sensibility, its confusion, for
example, its inarticulateness and precipitancy.
They form an ideal saxophone-music. Few
poets have rendered as immediately effects of
intense loudness, swiftness, brightness. Certainly, few Americans have revealed a vein of
melody as rich even in its facilenesses, and
produced singing lines as long and as exciting
in their convolutions. Besides, Cummings
finds himself momentarily in the main poetic
tradition; he has spoken out in the grand style
with some native magnificence; and one finds
him giving new life to traditional forms and
bird, flower and legendary themes. As brilliantly crowned with edge as *The Enormous
Room*, Cummings' first poetic collection assuredly is not. The prose is sustainedly clear
and positive of accent, and finely modulated,

but the poems, with all their evidences of the
sacred fire, their *diablerie* and whimsicality,
suggest an impulse less robustly taut and
integrated. The style is more abrupt in its
transitions. It borders sometimes upon inor-
ganity. The gift is to be found assuming easy
shapes; again and again his emotion appears
to elude the author. It is inadmissible that
Cummings felt no more than meets the ear
in certain places. Of conscious trickery there
is indeed no question; one merely feels at instances that the poet has disappeared, and
a prodigious frigid mechanism come to take
his place. Then, the qualifying adverbs grow
a little wearisome; the fervent Chopinesque
lyricism of the earlier work goes a little
rancid; while the coolness, sharpness, macabre
quality of the more permanently attractive
later poems wears a wilful air. Still, Cummings lean like Cummings fatter is an open
creature. No modern American poet save
Carl Sandburg has given himself as directly,
or shown as much veritable exuberance. If
the completely satisfactory line is to be found
more frequently in Cummings than the completely satisfactory poem, some bit of sharp
expressivity, some bit of color or melody

manages to get out into nearly every piece, and in numerous instances a great purity of feeling finds a voice. Many of the sonnets, impressions, and love-poems are full of a touching un-American spirit of youth, marvelously tender and young. Moreover, Cummings' theory of the printed word appears essentially sounder than Apollinaire's. It is closer to Mallarmé's; for the typographical display exists upon his pages never in the intention of picture-writing, and always for the purpose of marking the accelerations and hesitations of the rapid, capricious melodic line, and reinforcing the sense.

Very likely, should Cummings try himself out against a narrative, a most distinguished success would come to him, and his poetical achievement equal his work in prose. It is noteworthy that where he has a story to tell, a scene to set, he responds quite inspiredly: *Post-Impression No. 6* and *At the ferocious phenomenon of 5 o'clock* show his nervous notation at its best; and only a failure in mechanics, in stanza three, mars the episode in white inscribed *Of Nicolette.*

Cummings may prove a formidable sport from the old Puritanic stem. Members of

younger generations, literary and profane
alike, are not generally youthful in this young
country. Recruits for the career of letters,
for example, are most often "intellectuals,"
poor of trust in life, furnished with a culture
chiefly acquired in the manner of Beotia inside the library among encyclopedias, and involved in making the head alone perform what
cannot be achieved without the intermission of
the heart. Occasionally, as in all the provinces of life, the individual obedient to the
promptings of the senses, and exuberant and
magnanimous, does put in his appearance
among literary men; and something of the
beat of what exists gets into poem or story.
Unfortunately, too frequently these open na-
tures arrive unsustained by reading acquired
during the years when reading nourishes
most; and the taste for pure and accomplished
forms never erects itself strongly in them;
and in mid-career the mental tissue wears a
trifle thin. The fresh and generous spirit
possessed of his proper line of interest
among the materials of the earth, and given
an imperishable dream by Marlowe and Frois-
sart, Swinburne and Keats, is the rarest of all
esthetic phenomena. Yet E. E. Cummings,
we begin to observe, is such a one.

JAMES OPPENHEIM

JAMES OPPENHEIM

IN their incertitude, the members of the Seven Arts group over-rationalized the process of artistic creation. Literature, painting and music were going to be produced, it would have seemed, out of the impulse to rectify American life; and the summons to youth was couched too frequently in the shape of moral exhortations and appeals to the conscious will. The lady was charged to arise from the bed of her paralysis. Hence, one of the early issues of the magazine held an attack on Walter Lippman; for that which attacks and the thing attacked are often of a piece.

In certain of the members of the rebel group, the moralistic rationalizing attitude flowed from a state of weakness since rapidly left behind by them. But in others, the incapacity to permit a form, idea, or picture to speak for them has spoiled much of the work done by them in the days successive to the collapse of the young periodical; and among these latter James Oppenheim stands eminent. The

process of liberation has been a lingering one
for him. He has remained pretty consistently
on that somewhat mentally circumscribed and
rootless plane from which the entire group
commenced functioning. Much respectable
work has come out of him since the fall of
1917. He has waxed more powerful a mason
of words, and produced splendid bits of verbal
color and well-sustained passages of Whit-
manesque rhapsody. And many aspects
recommend him to his contemporaries, not
less appealingly now than in the past. As a
personality, he has proven himself always
kindly, paternal and sympathetic, possessed
of that alertness to world-issues, that sense
of values and largeness of outlook produced
by the stimulated intelligence. In every crisis
he has sided against the herd and with the
angels. But in his poetry, the rationalizing
habits: propaganda, self-reference, false generalization and the others which invariably
accompany uncertain feelings, have consistently bound him. If the better portion of his
work recently collected in the large volume
The Sea shows Oppenheim a maker of magnificent phrases, it also attests him predominantly a kind of exalted, dithyrambic Felix

Adler: exhorter and not artist. Only the more recent section of his work called *Golden Bird* brings evidence of feelings given something even vaguely approximating freedom.

It is not without a sentiment of the horrid irony of life that one sees in James Oppenheim a little "father of ethics." No writer has preached more vehemently, more consistently than he the necessity of creating out of pure unrationalized feeling and in disregard of past, received experience, nor attempted more grandiosely to express the subconscious uncharted elements of his own life. He has been very forward with the Mother, to utilize a little the language favored by some of his Jungian co-religionists when describing the mystic creative act, and pretended that he has produced from out his psyche many "fiery symbols" beyond himself. But it is only apparently that feeling maintains an equality with theory, to say nothing of primacy. The poetic sea rises in Oppenheim and cannonades against the cliffs. But never does the liquid matter become solidified in the form of a self-sufficient, self-manifest thing, no more than the winter sea itself becomes the cliffs whose shapes it momentarily seems to hold. The lyricism moves almost entirely within a pattern laid deliberately and from without upon it. The poet advances, tearing his priestly robes and spilling drunken language. Should you peer close, however, you would see the ecstasy gyrating inside a field delimited and staked out for it by a gray awake old reason; reason with its formulæ and preconceptions and psychoanalytical theories had arrived on the battle-ground long before poor sluggard feeling was up, and laid out the scene, the cold old thing, in conformity with laws abstracted from past experience. *Songs for the New Age* and *The Song of Life, The Mystic Warrior* and *The Solitary* alike, show emotions made to conform to some preconceived interpretation, and rattling about homelessly inside this arbitrarily imposed framework. Few scenes of the autobiographic *Mystic Warrior* are really felt. The poet has let only three or four of them become bitingly real to him. The greater number of the sections resemble statements far more than realizations. Nor are they permitted to talk for themselves, not even in their castrated condition. The author seems to have been afraid that the reader might see more than he was intended to see.

Each section in some corner includes a little *fabula docet.* Apparently at six Oppenheim met some dirty little boys, who gave him sticky cocoanut candy to eat; that night, his mother asked him to draw, and he began to design a sailor on a mast; then vomited: "So here," says the poet,

"is a curious beginning of that conception and giving birth
Which later shall be my art."

At twenty-seven he strikes up a friendship with a fellow poet, and on the Palisades they lie and talk. The scene we do not see, or hear the talk. It is the comment of the poet we get:

"We have recovered one of the secrets of the Periclean Greeks
The love of man for man which is rooted in the body
But raised into contactless talk."

Yet for some reason, *mirabile dictu,* we are not at all convinced that Oppenheim and his speech-friend really discovered the secret of the Periclean Greeks; and smile delightedly when rhetorically he demands:

"Did the Mermaid hear such things? the Grove of Athens?
Did Goethe and Schiller speak thus together?"

It becomes obvious very early that the author
is far less interested in the object before him
than in substantiating a preconception he en-
tertains concerning himself, the theory that he
has had if not the universal experience entire,
at least the experience from which great poetry
flows; and that he is to be compared to Walt
Whitman. He speaks of "the Walts and the
James's."

Like *The Mystic Warrior,* the narrative
poem *The Song of Life* and the drama *Night*
are built by means of rationalizations about the
person of the author. They reveal impulses of
self-justification and the necessity of calling a
mediocre experience by loud and august names
and reveal the ancient stratagem of the false
generalization. Oppenheim has not been able
to tie himself down to a specific. He dodges
nervously between "objectivity" and "subjec-
tivity," willing to fix on neither. The characters of the narrative poem remain dolls
prettily decorated, and move through Arthur
Davies' landscapes; the tale has neither
the naïveté of fiction nor the penetration
of philosophy. The play introduces a priest
who is no priest, a scientist not a scientist, and
a poet who could never in all the world write

a poem. *The Song of the Sea* is a rationalization also. It is true it commences as a metaphor, and moves grandiosely for a few pages. Nevertheless, we are made aware very shortly that the author gets not enough satisfaction out of feeling life through a thing. He has, it seems, to mount the orator's rostrum in person and exhort, declare and save. The music was merely a pretext, a sort of overture to a modern Junganalytic sermon.

Like content, like form. The surface of Oppenheim's work shows him possessed of no extraordinary sensitivity to the objects before him. The utterly living touch is out of his song. There are fresh informal perceptions on every page of Whitman; but Oppenheim's perceptions are always a little second handed. Sometimes he comes very close to capturing new sensations:

"The sea, black in the winter cloud-light,
  Swinging rough squares of sheeted water, laced with
    white foam,
  And spouting spume through the wind's mouth, and
    slashing into blue about jutting rocks,
Hard, broken, like jostling steel out to the sky-
    rim——"

and yet, one finds it difficult to feel a perfect crispness, immediacy. His poetic language

smells of the lamp; he knows Nietzsche, the
Song of Songs and Whitman not wisely but
too well. And if music comes to him readily, the tone of his speech remains ever a little
unmodulated and heavy and unrelieved. He
requires it seems an orchestra of a hundred
instruments to serenade his mistress, and the
exaltation finally wearies one. The really
lovely lyrics called *Songs out of Solitude,*
with their comparative reticency and subtlety
of mood, come like poultices

> To heal the blows of sound.

These songs, and the other unlabored pieces,
are islands in the sea; and something which
looks like the mainland seems to have appeared
in *Golden Bird.* The poet has finally gotten a
glimmer of the unconscious wisdom of Siegfried; for Brunhilde is never to be awaked with
exhortations or even with the perfectest ex-
position of the working of the psyche, and only
with a kiss. In many of the poems of this final
section of his completed work, Oppenheim has
given his lyrical moments with a minimum of
rationalization; he has sung in trust of his feelings, contented in singing; and kept his intellect fairly successfully from its habitual

interferences. These love-poems have a new subtlety, tenderness and incisiveness. And yet, *Golden Bird* remains a promise more than a satisfactory performance. It is never poetry of a very pellucid water. The kerosene of the library lamp remains faintly sensible; and *The Great Mother* is a shameless rationalization and *Hebrews* begins mightily and then dribbles into tawdry witticism. Hence, if these poems give one greater hope for Oppenheim's eventual freedom than one has dared for long to cherish, he has still to prove that he can root himself in the difficult coast land upon which he has at length set foot.

F. SCOTT FITZGERALD

F. SCOTT FITZGERALD

T HE utmost that can be charged against F.
Scott Fitzgerald is that too oftentimes
his good material eludes him. Of the ultimate
value of said material there is no dispute. Certain racehorses run for the pure joy of running, and the author of *The Beautiful and
Damned* and *Tales of the Jazz Age* is such
an animal. He is the born writer, amusing
himself with tales and pictures; and eventually
nothing is interesting except natural bent.
Salty and insipid, exaggeratedly poetical and
bitterly parodistic, his writing pours exuberantly out of him. Flat paragraphs are re-
deemed by brilliant metaphors, and conventional descriptions by witty, penetrating turns.
Ideas of diamond are somewhat indiscrimi-
nately mixed with ideas of rhinestone and ideas
of window glass; yet purest rays serene are
present in veritable abundance. They must
come to this bannerman of the slickers and flappers in a sort of dream, unexpectedly out of
some arcana where they have been concealing

themselves, and surprise him by smiling up at
him from underneath his pen.　For so they
startle the reader, unprepared to encounter in
writing as carelessly undertaken, ideas so mature and poignant and worthy of fine settings.

Not a contemporary American senses as
thoroughly in every fiber the tempo of privi-
leged post-adolescent America.　Of that life,
in all its 'great hardness and equally curious
softness, its external clatter, movement and
boldness, he is a part; and what he writes re-
flects the environment not so much in its superficial aspects as in its pitch and beat.　He
knows how talk sounds, how the dances feel,
how the crap-games look.　Unimportant detail
shows how perfect the unconscious attunement: the vignette of a boy drawing gasolene
out of an automobile tank during a dance so
that a girl can clean her satin shoe; the vignette
of a young fellow sitting in his B.V.D.'s after
a bath running his hand down his naked shin
in indolent satisfaction; the vignette of two
bucks from a pump-and-slipper dance throw-
ing hash by the handful around Childs' at six
A.M.　Not another has gotten flashes from the
psyches of the golden young intimate as those
which amaze throughout *The Beautiful and*

Damned. And not another has fixed as mercilessly the quality of brutishness, of dull indirection and degraded sensibility running through American life of the hour.

Taken as things, nevertheless, both the novels of Fitzgerald, and the majority of his tales as well, lie on a plane inferior to the one upon which his best material extends. He has the stuff for pathos, and this fact he fairly consistently ignores. Certain preconceptions seem to intrude between him and his material, spoiling his power to correctly appreciate it. Hence, instead of the veritable stories he has to tell, there appear smart social romanzas and unhappy happy endings. Of Fitzgerald's preconceptions, the chief sinner appears to be the illusion that the field of his vision is essentially the field of "youth." Now, it would be insanity to deny the author's almost constant preoccupation with exquisite creatures in chiffon and their slender snappy companions, or to deny the jolly subjects of his observations vivacity and frankness of spirit, and perfect elegance of texture. There is a place where an eternal dance proceeds, and this place for the while they occupy, filling it with their proper motions and gestures. And whatever the quality of these, who can for even an instant maintain that it is inferior to that of the dreadful motions and gestures which filled it a generation, or two or three generations ago? What one does affirm, however, and affirm with passion, is that the author of *This Side of Paradise* and of the jazzy stories does not sustainedly perceive his girls and men for what they are, and tends to invest them with precisely the glamour with which they in pathetic assurance rather childishly invest themselves. At the time of the appearance of Fitzgerald's first book, it was evident that to an extent he was indebted to Compton Mackenzie for the feeling with which he regarded the "dreaming spires" of Princeton; and since then it has become apparent that he tends a trifle overmuch to view everything which he sees in the light of Europe's past experiences. His protagonists he observes through the enchanted eyes of a perpetual Maytime, perceiving among the motors and crapgames a wave of cool spring flowers, a flutter of white and yellow ephemeridae. Even when he marks the cruel and shabby side, the decay and the ignobility of his objective, he tends to overplay the general attractiveness more than the detail warrants.

The couple in *The Beautiful and Damned,*
charming and comely enough and yet por-
trayed at length in the horrible effort to per-
petuate a state of narcissistic irresponsibility,
we are begged to perceive as iridescently wonderful bodies and souls.

And it is fresh, juicy and spontaneous that
the American juveniles of the class described
by Fitzgerald exactly are not. Superficially,
perhaps. But was not the forest green which
Europe called by the name of youth somewhat
more a thing of courage? And the number of
us willing to face the world without the pan-
oply of elaborate material protections is not
overwhelming. It is claimed that in the American South virgins are carefully trained to
inquire out the income and prospects of suitors,
and nip in the bud any passion which threatens
to direct itself upon an unworthy object. But
it does not seem probable there is any truth in
the report. For such maneuvers can scarcely
be necessary. It is undoubtedly physically impossible for any really nice American girl
South or North to respond to the desires of a
male who does not make the spiritual gesture paralleling the Woolworth Building's.
Through either external persuasion or inherent

idealism, and which it is we know not, and undoubtedly it is both, the self-respecting damsels
early acquire the conviction that splendidly
complete orientation onto the business of
material increase is the primary characteristic
of maleness, and that any offer of love unaccompanied by the tautness for money is
the profoundest of insults to the psyche seated
in the tender depths of them. And the strap-
ping, college-bred, Brooks-clad youths no less
than they share this beautiful innate belief.
They too seem unable to face life without having at the back of them the immense upholstery
of wealth. Nothing which they might be or do,
were they relieved of the necessity of being a
worldly success, appears to them capable of
making good to the lady the absence of the fur
garment and the foreign roadster, and the
presence of inevitable suffering. Thus the
spirit of the business world is established well
before the advent of puberty; and the spirit of
business is compromise, which is not exactly
it would seem the spirit of youth.

And even the lightest, least satirical of Fitzgerald's pages bear testimonial to the preva-
lence of the condition. A moralist could gather
evidence for a most terrible condemnation of

bourgeois America from the books of this protagonist of youth. And yet, *Lieb Vaterland, magst ruhig sein*. It is not a state of immorality in the general sense of the word that might be uncovered. If by morality we mean obedience to the *mores* of the tribe, then Fitzgerald's diverting flappers and slickers are in no sense licentious. By means of necking parties and booze fights of the sort he describes the republic is maintained. Business rests on them. But immorality may be taken to signify a falling away from the ideal spirit of life, and in that sense America is proven the breeding ground of a kind of decay. In all unconsciousness Fitzgerald shows us types of poor golden young too shallow to feel, vainly attitudinizing in the effort to achieve sensation: girls who know they cannot live without riches and men perpetually sucking the bottle for solace. The people aren't young; they are merely narcissistic. Knowledge of life is gotten from books, and the naïveté is not quite lovely. That is all very well; one has no fault to find with it; it is quite sanitary and not at all messy as passion usually is; but why call it spring? And occasionally Fitzgerald drops the light guitar and with cool ferocity speaks the veritable name.

May Day, perhaps the most mature of all his tales, brings the bitter brackish dry taste of decay fully to the mouth. With an air of almost glacial impersonality Fitzgerald gives a curious atmosphere of mixed luxury and rottenness of the heart. Through the entire story there seems to run the brutishness of the two soldiers hiding among pails and mops in the dust closet waiting for some stolen liquor to be handed in to them. And in the fantasia *The Diamond Big as the Ritz,* Fitzgerald strikes perhaps quite undeliberately further notes of satire: Mr. Braddock Washington, the richest and most profoundly unsympathetic man in the world looks dangerously like a jazz-age portrait of the father of the country.

But the world his subject-matter is still too much within Fitzgerald himself for him to see it sustainedly against the universe. Its values obtain too strongly over him, and for that reason he cannot set them against those of high civilizations, and calmly judge them so. Hence, wanting philosophy, and a little over-eager like the rest of America to arrive without having really sweated, he falls victim to the favorite delusions of the society of which he is a part, tends to indulge it in its dreams of grandeur, and misses the fine flower of pathos. He seems to set out writing under the compulsion of vague feelings, and when his wonderfully revelatory passages appear, they come rather like volcanic islands thrown to the surface of a sea of fantasy. By every law *The Beautiful and Damned* should have been a tragedy, the victims damned indeed; yet at the conclusion Fitzgerald welched, and permitted his pitiful pair to have the alleviations of some thirty millions of dollars, and his hero tell the readers he had won out. To be sure, a steady growth has been going on within this interesting author. The amusing insolence of his earlier manner of writing has persistently given away before a bolder, sharper stroke less personal in reference. The descriptions in *May Day:* the sight of the avenue, the drinking scene in Delmonico's, the adventures of Mr. In and Mr. Out, are done with quiet virtuosity. A very genuine gift of fantasy arrives in *Benjamin Button.* There are even Lawrence-like strong moments in *The Beautiful and Damned.* And still, in spite of *May Day,* Fitzgerald has not yet crossed the line that bounds the field of art.

He has seen his material from its own point of view, and he has seen it completely from without. But he has never done what the artist does: seen it simultaneously from within and without; and loved it and judged it too. For *May Day* lacks a focal point, and merely juxtaposes a number of small pieces. Should Fitzgerald finally break his mold, and free himself of the compulsions of the civilization in which he grew, it might go badly with his popularity. It will be a pathetic story he will have to tell, the legend of a moon which never rose; and that is precisely the story a certain America does not wish to hear. Nevertheless, we would like hugely to hear him tell it. And Fitzgerald might scarcely miss his following.

JEAN TOOMER

JEAN TOOMER

MOMENTARILY the prose of *Cane* is artificially exalted, hooked to the Frankian pitch as to a nail high up in the wall. And night is the soft belly of a pregnant negress, and "her mind" a pink mesh bag filled with baby toes. But quickly the inflations subside. The happy normal swing resumes, the easy rhythm of a strainless human frame.

Not all the narratives intend the quality of legendary song. Certain give the fragmentated moods of the contemporary psychic conflict, and throb with hysterical starts and tearing dissonance. Yet saving the few derailing exaltations, the swing and balance of the limber body walking a road is ever-present. The musical state of soul seems primary in Jean Toomer. The pattern generates the tale. He tunes his fiddle like a tavern minstrel, and out of the little rocking or running design there rises the protagonist, solidifying from rhythm as heroes once solidified from mist: crouched whitewoman Becky who had two negro sons;

Carma in overalls and strong as any man; Kabnis with his jangling nerves and flooding nostalgic lyricism. The rhythm forms the figures most. The words are but flecks of light gleaming on the surface of bronze.

He has his hand lightly, relaxedly, upon substances. The words transmit the easy sensations. They come warm and fuzzy and rich not with the heat and density of bodies crowded in tenements, but with the level beat of a blood promenaded in resinous forests amid blotches of June sun on needles and cones. It is the "sawdust glow of night" and the "velvet pine-smoke air." "The sun which has been slanting over her shoulder, shoots primitive rockets into her mangrove-gloomed, yellow flower face." He assembles words as a painter negligently rubbing pastels; leaving where he touches warm singing blobs of brown and red.

There are no rings laming this imagination, most the time: and binding it in on his proper person. Toomer's protagonists, symbols and situations are not of the nature of prearrangements: objects glued together on a mental plane and revealing through wooden joints and inner dislocation the artificial synthesis. His creative power offers to bring this young poet-novelist high in the ranks of living American letters. Characters and narratives move, and move in unpremeditated, unpredictable curves. Yet in their sudden tangential departures and radical developments they remain logical with a logic profounder than the intellect's. Not all the personages and situations of the stories, it is true, are submitted to extended composition and developed. The majority remain exposed in a single scene and through a single view. Yet in the nouvelle *Kabnis* Toomer has produced an extended composition. The focal character is moved through several episodes, and with each episode the scope of the story deepens. Characters and situations are satisfying both as symbol and as fact; and toward the conclusion both are transposed without violence to a level of reality deeper than that upon which they were launched. Possibly the upper conscious level of mind alone could have produced the earlier scenes; they may be semi-autobiographical, and felt with the aid of Sherwood Anderson and *The Portrait of the Artist as a Young Man*. But not the fantastic scene in the cellar, with its opposition of the torn differentiating negroids and the figure of

the ancient African slave mumbling in his
corner. Some inner substance in the author
moved while writing this tale. He was no
longer the same man who began it, when writing the end. He had stepped on a level of
pure invention.

Toomer's free gift has given him the vision
of a parting soul, and lifted his voice in salu-
tation to the folk-spirit of the negro South.
He comes like a son returned in bare time to
take a living full farewell of a dying parent;
and all of him loves and wants to commemo-
rate that perishing naïveté, only beautiful one
America has had, before universal ugly sophistication cover it also. Those simple singing
people who have joy and have pain, and voice
them frankly, largely, utterly have come to
hold for him a great earthly beauty and
tragedy. Their sheer animal litheness and
pathos has become savage and satisfying to
his breast:

A feast of moon and men and barking hounds
An orgy for some genius of the South
With blood-hot eyes and cane lipped scented mouth—

He follows the elasticity, resiliency of young
rubber, into the brown belt of Washington:
feels it in its conflict with the sophistication

and mechanization of white America; watches it weakened and threatened and torn in the bodies of self-conscious, half-educated people, girls become self-centered and men playing the piano in vaudeville theatres and going dreaming of Walt Whitman under the lamps of Seventh Street. And here he perceives, like new strange harmonies sounding through the subtle dissonances of life, promises of an inner healing for these splintered souls, a new strength, swiftness and singleness of motive. A new soul calls. The negroid poet of the story pulled from his base by the wilfulness of a passionate white girl, half lets his amorous opportunity pass in a proud gesture of balladry. Through the woof of *Kabnis* there go the figures of Lewis and Carrie; and Lewis is a man who has become fearless and self-confident and fine; and Carrie is a girl in whom has persisted flowerlike a beauty of instinct.

But these figures are prophetic not only for men of negro blood. They throw forward much in America; for they are symbols of some future America of which Jean Toomer by virtue of the music in him is a portion. He looks two ways. Through this recognition of the beauty of a doomed simplicity some simplicity, sensuosity, passionateness not of the South or of the past asserts, cries out, comes conscious of itself: some America beyond the news-papers, regimented feelings, edgeless lan-guage—timid, uncertain, young—in streaming music nevertheless drawing more imminent.

Both Anderson and Frank have helped rouse the impulse of Toomer. Yet it was the imag-ists with their perfect precision of feeling that fevered him most for work. Some clarity in himself must have responded to the clearness of these poets. That his definiteness remains as yet less intense than theirs is plain. Per-haps because his gift is warmer and more tubulent, it is also less white and clear. What-ever the cause, the Frankian inflations, and the wobbling of the focus between Kabnis and Lewis in the finale of the novelette, leave the indecision a little plainer than we would have it. Large as is the heralding which comes through him, Toomer remains as yet much of the artist trying out his colors, the writer ex-perimenting with a style. And still, these movements of prose are genuine and new. Again a creative power has arrived for Ameri-can literature: for fiction, perhaps for criticism; in any case, for prose. Other writers have tried, with less happiness, to handle the material of the South. They have had axes to grind; sadisms to exhaust in whipping up passion for the whites; masochisms to release in waking resentment for the blacks. But Toomer comes to unlimber a soul, and give of its dance and music.

HERBERT J. SELIGMANN

HERBERT J. SELIGMANN

ERBERT SELIGMANN possesses a
highly developed sense of pitch. He has
the rare faculty of ascertaining with nicety
the quality, force and timbre of the novel or
painting, the symphony or personality, to
which he has been exposed, and crystallizing
it coolly in a sentence or a phrase. Only yesterday he told us that Ronald Firbank's
Prancing Nigger was Rabelais reduced to the
scale of Mr. Crowninshield's *Vanity Fair;* and
somewhere he describes Hartley as a young
man "writing his preferences somewhat
grandly across the face of the universe." If
the nuggets drop from him perhaps more lib-
erally in conversation than in composition, no
piece of critical writing done by him, no newspaper article even, is bare of the swift true perceptions from which sharply living pictures
are to be developed; and all his work, despite
its fragmentariness, indicates immediate relationship to something in the universe. His
monograph on D. H. Lawrence, perhaps the

most elaborate piece of writing attempted by him, parallels momentarily with a closeness that is dazzling the gesture of the English agonist. And though at present Seligmann is the much-needed unrationalistic critic more in embryo than in figure, the increasing frequency and consequentiality of his spark-like relationship with things, and the increasing freshness and freedom of his phrase, promise a proximate emergence. No sense of pitch comes unaccompanied by a sense of flow; and Seligmann, to do finely sustained and ordered prose, has merely, it appears, to hearken a little more closely than he has hitherto done to the rhythms knocking at him in hours of excitement.

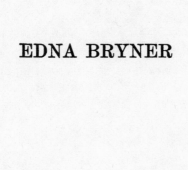

EDNA BRYNER

EDNA BRYNER

YOU could guess Edna Bryner has more German than Anglo-Irish blood in her veins. The feeling for forests which she shows in her stories, and for the minds of those who dwell under their boughs, betrays the descent. She heard no German in her home; she has never been conscious of any relationship to any earth other than American. Yet no descendant of purely insular stock could develop, as we assured, quite her love of trees and perceptivity of their looks, the spread of their foliage and the quality of the life led underneath them. It is not in the blood. The great forests were gone from the British Isles before the emigration westward began. And the life developed in America has not been careful of trees. Forests have been devastated, let burn down, and made into— newspapers. Climate, soil, and watersupply, alike have suffered. America may yet share the fate of Spain. But love of the tree is planted deep in German blood. The intensity of the relationship is expressed alike in actuality and idea. You find it demonstrated in the magnificent care given by the German to his forest-lands and in the singular harmony of his word *Der Wald;* in the charmingly habitual tramping-tours and in such familiar ideal expressions as the lyricism of Eichendorff, the horns of the *Freischütz* overture, and the mood of the first two acts of *Siegfried.* And doubtless, like so many offshoots of continental stocks, incessantly impelled to bring latent inherent strengths into relationship with American life, Miss Bryner has found a curious release in expressing her feeling about the woods and telling truly the careers of Mountain Minds and Forest Dwellers in their native wildernesses and out in the open and the flat and the crowded.

There is no tendency in this writing, no deliberate relationship of esthetic problems to the economic problem of reforestation. If you should ask Miss Bryner what it is the question means to her, she would doubtless reply in some surprise and with much amusement, "What is the sense of life if a tree doesn't grow?" It is merely that she has feelings about the abstract thing which we call life,

and again and again finds herself quite un-
rationalizingly expressing it through stories in
which the forest plays a rôle. The forest for
her is really an idea, an imaginative projection
of the inmost self, a means of focusing
through a beloved and common thing, the
values of existence. It appears that the father
of Edna Bryner, whose people had been
charcoalburners in Saxony, during a portion
of her childhood was a lumberman in the
Pennsylvania woods, and tragically mistook
the American profession of lumberman for
the profession which his ancestors called the
forester's. In the most impressionable portion of her life, therefore, she felt the conflict
between European culture and American vandalism, without realizing precisely what it was
that was going on about her; felt the fine feeling for an impersonal thing communicated to
her by her father being discarded by the life
involving them all. Hence, it was natural that
in the hour when she, as a matured woman,
found her own superior impersonal attitude
toward things in conflict with the inferior personal attitude of American society, she should
find herself for a while returning to the source
of the conflict in herself, discovering the roots

of her feelings, and continuing, on the plane of idea, but in its own terms her father's hopeless fight. The tree has become a symbol. Behind it, there seems to stand the series of generous nature, generous people, community, the life of the race. The love of trees is merely the gate.

It seems she is one of the women who have very safely come through the movement for Women's Rights. The movement was a necessity ten years since. To-day, its ideals are antiquated. One smiles at the women still minimizing the difference between the sexes. The new ideal is not competitive. In Miss Bryner, one finds it asserting itself in an affirmative way through an impersonal attitude toward the materials of existence, and in a negative through the rejection of the type of womanhood which persists in feeling itself as the unique vessel of the world-soul. That is why so many of her stories expose with perfect realism women whose veritable feeling never quite manages to transcend their own persons, and who try tragically in their conceit to make the intellect perform what only the heart is capable of doing. Assuredly, the movement of which she is a portion has merely begun its march. Her forms of expression are not always smooth. She is oftentimes found in intensest struggles with her medium. But what she has already expressed has strength of conception, shows first-hand knowledge of people, and is informed by a perfectly realistic attitude toward life. She takes her place among those women who, engaged in the arts, have to communicate a staunch and lovely life of feeling.

EMILE VERHAEREN

EMILE VERHAEREN

VERHAEREN brought into poetry a Flemish gorgeousness turned black. He was the rude, the vehement, the exalted workman in French verse, twisting words and rhythms in his vast hands as though they were metal bars, kneading them into solid, broad and heavily colored beauty. He was blood-brother to the drunken Flanders brushmen who splashed hot summer light onto their canvases and rioted in carnal dreams of breasts and satins, meats and flagons; save that in him their own grand red achieved at first climaxes in the lower scale only, and took form in violent states of depression and writhings of impotence and pain. The earliest of Verhaeren's volumes, it is true, stands a glorification of the robust art of the kermess-painters and the sappy flesh of their women; but this book *Les Flamandes,* like its successor *Les Moines,* is essentially external. The idiom is not Verhaeren's own, for it is borrowed from the arts of the past. The form is Parnassian; perversely so; Verhaeren

has merely substituted for the china vases and
Sicilian coins of Gautier and Heredia the vulgar world of Steen and Breughel, and used its
traits in forming a sensible and exterior
beauty. And the feeling is nostalgic, fugitive
from the objects surrounding the poet. His
being is a-yearn from the present back into a
"time" when breasts were firm and loins in-
defatigable, and when the Catholic faith was
real in men. With a sort of wonder he stands
before the gross victuals and furious potations
and big cod-pieces of the past, or dreams himself into the dead world of medieval mysticism.
Only in the time of *Les Soirs* and *Les Dé-
bâcles* and *Flambeaux Noirs* did Verhaeren
leave fantasy-making, feel himself through
his own circumstance, and develop his proper
idiom; and these his first fully authentic works
are the expression of a rich vitality unable to
gather headway and release itself in joy and
abundance of satisfactions and labors, and
turned destructively against its possessor. Robust clashfulness has become the grinding of
harsh protesting words; broadness of rhythm a
painful monotony; exaltation and drunkenness
a flow of fearful and depressive music. The
poems reflect the weak melancholy of an hun-

dred endless Sunday evenings through which the tower-bells toll funereally. The old Flemish splendor is still present, and brings the symbols of solid substantial things; but the breasts swollen with sap and the banquets and scarves and banners have become hard, glittering, sinister: cold rock, cold steel, snow, silver, ice, and the shadows of moony winter landscapes.

Some faith in life, some power of love, could not establish itself. Verhaeren had the modern malady of fear, for he was the born lover unable to find the direction of life in the terrible, ultramodern day. The old religious spirit, which had bound men to each other and made it possible for them to project beyond themselves a picture of a better order, was dead. The old forms of life, the old habits, the old values, Pan and Jesus both were dead with it. The very landscape had changed. Flanders had undergone during the first half of the nineteenth century a transformation almost necromantic. A somnolent agricultural and small manufacturing country had of a sudden become a furnace. Vast manufacturing cities were sucking up the rural populations. Nature had taken shapes of brick and glass and steel.

The individual was tinier than ever before the new aggregations of power, the new massings of humanity. He was the plaything of new incommensurable forces, new demons and new gods.

And this strange present demanded the love of man! demanded that he relinquish his old modes of apprehension, be born in harmony with the new order, affirm it, venture forth with it on its voyage into the unknown, cleave to it for ill or good. So only might he come to the complete enjoyment of his faculties. That was the universal challenge, to poet and layman. And Verhaeren's acceptation of the challenge, his first long abortive efforts to synchronize with the new rhythms of life, are in those poems of dark crucifixion. They are the expression of neurasthenia, of the malady of an age; and picture in their rhythms and clashings, their frantic cries and sinister coloring the neurasthenic's morbid attention to the activity of his own body, his wild self-forcings, and hysterical states of fear for his reason. Metal weights crush his head as under a stony crown. Weariness ties him down to his chair: the world is too black and too empty to be essayed; he is obsessed by the force of numbers, the geometrical flares of the universe. The poet knows a life is there from which he is prisoned, and claws vainly at his chains. A great deal of morbid curiosity has been excited by these poems, and Stefan Zweig, Verhaeren's German translator and apostle, believes that the poet was insane during the period they were composed. There is no doubt the man was sick to the point of suicide; for body and soul of the artist are one; and those who knew Verhaeren said that all his life his face showed signs of the sufferings he had undergone in this struggle for a hold on life. And emergence from under the hood of self was a process extended over a length of years: the life of Verhaeren was like the symphony of his compatriot Franck, an ascent from dark to light so gradual that at times it seems no progress upward is being made, and the black seems to thicken and the woeful cries to carry the burden of a more hopeless sorrow.

But, precisely as in the close of the symphony of Franck the bells of faith ring out slow and proud at last, and broad Flemish sunlight transfuses the orchestra, so in the career of Verhaeren did love of life and joy in its manifestations come finally to possess the man

entire. His latter volumes, *Les forces, tumul-
tueuse, La multiple splendeur, Les rhythmes
souveraines* are hymns of gladness. The world
has known some artists, it is true, who did not
have to make the long cruel progress toward
joy which this man had to make on hands and
knees. Born at the summit of *his* mountain of
purgatory; once-born, perhaps, their art was a
long, a mighty, a continual affirmation. But
there has been only one Rubens, only one Haen-
del, only one Rabelais. The greater number of
the affirmers have had to toil toward the state
of yea-saying to life, and most have died along
the way. But Verhaeren is of the company of
the conquerors. He came at last to stand
among the Titans, and Flanders splendor to
express itself again in positive statement.

It began, this synchronization in the rhythm
of the new time, with a curious half realistic,
half symbolical seeing of the white-bled countryside and the octopus-like, sucking city. In
these poems of his middle period, *Les Cam-
pagnes Hallucinées* and *Les Villes Tenta-
culaires,* Verhaeren gives, with sure grasp of
fact and equally sure ability to express the invisible elements of life in personifications, the
past and present side by side: the agricultural

past a brooding, miasmal ghost, the industrial
present a black jumble over rivers of pitch and
naphtha. But the new world is no longer
merely an overwhelming, baffling ugliness for
the poet. He does not shirk its crassness, its
inhumanity, its noisesomeness; and it commences pervading him with a feeling of power.
He sees the new gods of humanity *en masse,*
the new beings made of groups and aggregations of men. He sees the old gods and saints
become steamers, locomotives, banks, factories,
marts, laboratories. He knows that over the
brutal flaring roaring cities there brood nevertheless the ideas, and that a new spiritual
might has come to assert itself over mankind.
What matter then, it sang in him,

> Si quelque jour, du fond des brouillards et des voiles,
> Surgit un nouveau Christ, en lumière sculpté,
> Qui soulève vers lui l'humanité
> Et la baptise au feu de nouvelles étoiles?

And by the side of these rude and ardent
rhapsodies of the common life there stand,
proof additional that his emotions had found
a channel into the real stuff of the world, Verhaeren's poems of love. For these expressions
of intimacy *Les heures claires* and *Les
heures d'après-midi,* are testimonials of a

union silent and steadfast in which a whisper, a glance, a half-realized gesture, is language enough. In the stream of his exalted, clashful verse, they lie like some bird-haunted islet tranquil in sunshine.

Until at length the man who had fled from the new world came to hymn a humanity which, grown adjusted to its battleground of energies and finding the door of the ancient Eden open once more to it, refuses to forego the earth; and all the exultation and appetite latent in Verhaeren broke loose in vehement, sonorous verse. Rhythms spring and bound explosively. Words in orders which the Parisians disclaim for French, bite and flare with rude triumphant force. In these violent rhapsodies, there is all the yea-saying of the hearty sensuous Fleming hungry as in his great century for experience, for labor, for beauty, and inflamed by the palpable charm of the earthly life. They are crammed with the discovered wonder of the new engines and gods and horizons. The strutting life of the great ports and centers vibrates in them: the shipping, the factories, the gold, the railroads, the industrial aggregations, the dominating figures of captains and engineers and saints, the new ideas, the new discoveries,

the new dreams and fervors and religions. The
poems act like physical stimuli. Intoxication
wells in them. Verhaeren was deliberately the
poet of enthusiasm, setting out to fire men with
his dionysiac verse, to excite their imaginations
with the spectacle of modern life, so that they
might be impregnated with the creative impulse so ardent in himself. And, rhetorician,
sentimentalist, and child, he not unoften succeeds of his high purpose. For the man actually through faith had synchronized with the
stream carrying the future; and through that
touch got powers of communicating life. It
was no longer his small Belgium that limited
Verhaeren's sympathy by its borders. He had
arisen on the wave of a nationalistic literary
expression; but the deeper he penetrated life,
the farther beyond the borders of his country
did life carry his understanding. For a new
man was being molded by the power of the
modern mechanical devices, the obliteration of
distances, the knitting of peoples; and Verhaeren knew Antwerp and Cologne, Paris and
Düsseldorf, London and Milan as one; felt Europe as a whole and Europe and America as
one. And he spoke for the modern man and his
feverish system.

Je suis le fils de cette race
Dont les cerveaux plus que les dents
Sont solides et sont ardents
Et sont voraces.

Through him, there commenced to cry the abstract "beings greater than man" which fill the
world with their play, and give shape to the
new society; and inspiration gathered from
Whitman is passed on to Jules Romains.
Through Verhaeren, too, there spoke the mysticism of commerce; routes of trade giving the
ancient soul of man new frontiers, new colors:
experience of strange lands laying the foundation of a new consciousness and a new sympathy in the exclusive provincial human being;
and the route later to be explored by Johannes
Jensen was initiated.

It is a little difficult to-day to let the sovereign rhythms and high flames in upon one.
One dreads entrusting oneself to their positive
emotions! For everything which has occurred
in the decade since they were composed has
contradicted their vigorous affirmations. One
wonders whether Verhaeren during the black
years of the war did not feel that he had been
rudely awakened from a terrible insane
dream; one finds oneself speculating whether
the railway accident in which he met his

death in 1916 might not, after all, have
been suicide. For he had hymned the new
Europe and its godlike energy. And he saw
the energy transformed into a paroxysm of
self-destruction. He had felt himself not
less German than Belgian or French; in Germany they had hailed him a German poet who
by matter of chance wrote in the French language. And he saw Germany overrun Belgium
and a whole world revert to barbarism. How
deeply the man who had been signaled as conscience of his little country must have been
made to suffer in the universal night, we can
but guess. He had sung for all the world. In
all the world he had had faith. To all the
world his word had gone. And he must have
been torn apart by what he had to see; and
many a system stronger than his own suc-
cumbed to weariness. In one little work, perhaps his last, *Parmi les cendres,* the old faith
flickers a little. He dreams that Belgium, as
after the Burgundian, the Spanish, the Aus-
trian slavery, will re-arise; and that Europe is
being born afresh out of death. But the night
was endless; and it is not yet dawn, today.

And yet, shall we not finally have to give in
to this panmundane feeling after all? Verhae-

ren would have acquitted himself of insanity long since, had he been left among the living. For it is only in the feeling of which he became the great contemporary carrier that salvation lies for the world. Foredoomed to success or to failure, men will have to bring themselves to the effort of saving their habitation from ultimate ruin; and go the way, the only possible one, which his emotion blazed for them.

EDMOND ROSTAND

EDMOND ROSTAND

ROSTAND'S plays are artificial and conventional. Stale air of the playhouse pervades them. They are full of theatrical counterfeit and romantic fustian. The verse at best is pretty and clever, and in the main undistinguished and unmusical. Nevertheless, they had a reception extraordinary in the history of the stage. Their success was not simply a popular one. It was a literary success complete and world-wide. To many folk it seemed as if through Rostand poetic drama had rearisen; that through him a physically beautiful theater was to flourish once again. In electing him to membership and "immortality" the French Academy merely gave official sanction to the belief held by cultivated people not in France alone but the world over, that Edmond Rostand was a poet of originality and importance, and *Cyrano de Bergerac* a dramatic master-work.

Rostand was fortunate in the moment in which he appeared. Had it not been for the

condition of the French stage at the time of
their production, his dramas would never have
as completely imposed themselves. But in the
latter nineties the realistic theater—at least
the realistic theater as the Boulevards understood it—had become insupportable in its dulness. Originally the realistic departure had
been a movement toward restoring to the stage
its poetic and revelatory function. The facti-
tude, the utilization of elements abstracted
from contemporary society, was only part of
a general aversion from the unreality and con-
ventionality of the romantic stage toward a
form that should express indeed the modern
man. But in France the movement was not
directed by poets. It did not produce men of
the mastery and intelligence of Ibsen and
Strindberg. It never had full development.
It merely brought forward a comparatively
serious race of playwrights, men to an extent
aware of the forces of the world, but not eman-
cipated sufficiently to give them plastic expression. And so, instead of reforming the theater
it only succeeded in effecting a prosy compromise and creating the play of the social intention, the "problem play." The theater now
approximated the lecture hall. One visited it

to hear the statement of a doctrine, or to assist
at the discussion of a thing pretentiously
dubbed "problem." People wrote plays to
answer the questions "Should one get di-
vorced?" or "Should one forgive one's wife?"
or "What should a physician who infects a
patient with a fatal malady do?" And the
questions of conscience became more and more
tedious and academical, and the theses more
and more chilling, and the physicians and maladies more and more incredible. Then Rostand appeared with his Cyrano. And with
hearts overflowing with gratitude and with
cries of thanksgiving the whole of France went
to see his play.

For Rostand brought relief. He rid the public of the prosy social study and gave it instead
a theater-piece. Gone were the mouthing hus-
bands, the enigmatical wives, the diseases and
the doctors. Here, in place of the eternal
"problem" was a novel and piquant adventure; in place of the psychological grubbings,
"action" a-plenty. And for a generation
starved long enough by the charmlessness of
the theater, Rostand's play was most satisfying. Not only were the brilliant and romantic
setting, the brave and strange costumes, decor-

ative and exciting. The speech as well was
happier. The muddy and oratorical language
of Dumas fils, of de Curel, Hervieu and the rest
had been replaced by a gay and agreeable flow
of verse. Indeed, so strong was the purely external allure of Rostand's theater, the bright
and rapid business, the alternate lulling and
pricking of his verse, that it is small wonder it
it was overvalued, and that what indeed was a
regression was momentarily mistaken for a
reform.

For, if Rostand did bring relief, it was not
by attaining the goal of the social dramatists
and bringing poetry to the theater again. It
was rather by permitting the entire reform
movement to slip, and suffering the public to
snap back into the mental position from which
the realists had partly weaned it. As far as
the public went, the social drama had never
been more than a good habit half-heartedly
adopted. And Rostand let it indulge in the old
bad habit again. He gave it the old theatrical
counterfeit which it still craved, and there is
little falsehood as splendid of exterior as the
traditional "theater-play" of the French nation. He gave it the play built up out of the
conventions imposed upon the stage by the

vanity of generations of actors and the infantilism of generations of audiences. What he gave must not be confused with theatrical art; the art which communicates a superior sense of reality through a frank acceptance of the limits of the medium. It merely repeats the conventions of other theatric art as though they themselves were life, and not the facts made plastic by them. No doubt Rostand brought it forward well convinced that he had created the "new romance," the "new poetic drama." But he was a man quite innocent of sense of fact, and therefore unable to distinguish as affected and false what was merely routine in the theater. He thought that in *Les Romanesques* he had reflected *Romeo and Juliet,* and wilfully associated with Shakespeare's poetry a play that for all its "vers legers," its "robes claires," is merely the sermon of an elderly uncle. He wrote a *Princesse Lointaine* and calmly introduced into the very citadel of romance a Sardou heroine fresh from the dressing rooms; and placed in the mouth of chatelaine and troubadours a flood of rhetoric and rant in lieu of poetry. *Chantecler,* that might have been like one of those animal fables, full of mother-wit, found in the lore of every folk, is precious and virtuosic. And Cyrano himself, poor marionette, is the very strut and pose and gesture of the romantic melodrama assembled in one figure; Cyrano, who is decked out as the hero of the new poetic drama, and who gets up and declaims before falling dead, like a tenor in an Italian opera! And certainly the pith and core of Rostand's work, the verse, reveals an intelligence forever moving about his subject and glancing off from it, never for a moment entering into the matter and making it plastic. Instead of a single idea, he pours forth a hundred fancies; instead of a single trenchant image he gives precious and superficial associations. His verse never comes to have the directness and significance of veritable speech. Like his whole work, his whole consciousness, it is an evasion.

Hence, when *Chantecler* was produced it found a world grown indifferent, hostile even, to Rostand. It was not that the play represented a failure of craft. On the contrary, *Chantecler* is perhaps the most honest of all Rostand's plays. A certain sincerity and truthful feeling, however thin, does inform it. But the moment of Cyrano was gone. The play was judged with sobriety, perhaps even with

a certain malice: the revenge of men who had
permitted themselves to be deceived. And so
it fell flatter even than it deserved. No doubt
there are still plenty of people who cherish the
old mis-conception and find not only Cyrano
but the Duc de Reichstadt and the all too vocif-
erous cock heroic and deeply moving types.
But, in general, the verdict on *Chantecler* is the
verdict on Rostand. It contains the slightly
belated valuation of a work which was but one
of the many false dawns: even more void of the
art of the theater than the drama which it cast
into disfavor.

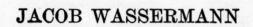

JACOB WASSERMANN

JACOB WASSERMANN

THE war has given many of us opportunity of discovering how truly we are "members one of another." Grimly comic indeed appears to-day the speech of the good Sunday-promenading citizen in "Faust":

Nichts Bessers weiss ich mir an Sonn- und Feiertagen
Als ein Gespräch von Krieg und Kriegsgeschrei,
Wenn hinten, weit, in der Türkei,
Die Völker auf einander schlagen.
Man steht am Fenster, trinkt sein Gläschen aus
Und sieht den Fluss hinab die bunten Schiffe gleiten;
Dann kehrt man Abends froh nach Haus,
Und segnet Fried' und Friedenszeiten

and the reply of his Sunday-promenading neighbor:

Sie mögen sich die Köpfe spalten,
Mag alles durcheinander gehn;
Doch nur zu Hause bleib's beim Alten.

For, since one man shot another in a Bosnian town, we have been discovering what the good burghers ignored, what good burghers never seem able to learn: that even though seated snugly within their walls, they and their children and their children's children are in mortal peril whenever war breaks out, even though it break out *hinten, weit, in der Türkei.* Before August, 1914, we too perhaps were a little prone to believe that what went on in neighboring houses was of no importance to us. Of importance alone, it seemed, was what was done in our own. Now, alas, we know that we are implicated not only in a battle in the Balkans, or in any even more distant portion of the globe, but in whatever is done by men whether in war or in peace, whether in Europe or in Africa, Australasia or South America. What men are about at this very moment, in Paris and Siberia, Mexico and Bombay; what men are about in a thousand spots of earth to which our attention has not as yet been directed by the news, may, now we know, change utterly the significance of our lives. We know that nothing is done on earth that is not done alike to all alive upon it; and not only alike to those alive upon it at present, but to those who once lived, and to those who have yet to come to birth upon its surface.

The discovery made since Sarajevo has helped to bring Dostoievsky closer. The sense of the terrible entanglement of existences is but the negative aspect of the great wisdom alive within the Russian novelist. What had been born in the breasts of the Hebrew prophets, and transferred by them to the primitive Christians, and been born again in Francis of Assisi, had found its latest high expression in him. Dostoievsky knew that we are, all of us, portions of a single greater man. He knew that a single substance, a single breath, is alike in all men, and that whatever is done to it is done to all. He knew that what seemed to be other folk was but oneself multiplied; that the murderer advancing to the judgment-bar to be sentenced was but oneself in another shape; that all men were equally guilty of every crime and equally innocent; that whosoever suffers, suffers not only because of himself, but because of and for all men; that whosoever expiates, expiates not only his own sins but those of all men. Though Smerdiakov commits the murder in *The Brothers Karamazov,* we are made to feel Mitia and Ivan equally guilty, and, since their father was what he was, equally innocent; Aliosha knows it, and takes upon himself voluntarily the punishment. At the close of *The Idiot,* after the assassination of Nastasia, the two men Muichkin and

Rogojin lie down on the floor together to sleep, and we know that the two, the saint and the assassin, are a single man. For Dostoievsky, too, there was no salvation for the race save through the Russian Christ; save through this sense of the unity of all men, of the common responsibility of all men, through this universal sympathy. Only on the day when folk ceased praying to God to save them individually, only when they ceased trying to save themselves individually through material aggrandizement, only on the day when a child was no longer "my child" or "your child," but when every child was recognized as a universal responsibility, would the dawn come for mankind.

In the breasts of the thousands upon thousands of men convinced by the war of the tragic interplay of existences, there must have been born, unbeknown to themselves, some hope of the advent of the Russian Christ, some faith that unless he came, the power of the white man, at least, would be shattered. This it is that the author of *Christian Wahnschaffe* comes to tell us. When, in the last dark years of the war, Jacob Wassermann found himself driven to his work-table, it was a vulgarization, in the good sense of the word, of the Russian novelist, that began forming in his mind. *The World's Illusion,* as the book is called by the English translator, shows, as does no other recent novel, the new light shed upon life by Dostoievsky. What Wassermann has sought to portray, in his two-volume romance, is nothing other than the new birth, in the breast of a man of our time, of the sense of the oneness of all people, of the sense that what alone matters is what lies between folk. In *Christian Wahnschaffe,* the hero of his ballad-novel—for the dryness and the rapidity of the narrative give the book a half movie-like, half archaic timbre—he has tried to create a Francis of Assisi of the dawning twentieth century. Like the "poor little man" of the Umbrian town, the modern Francis is born of gentle parents, shares in the best civilization of his time, and finds himself renouncing his parents and his patrimony in order to live in a *portiuncola,* in the Moabit district of Berlin. At the beginning of the romance, we find Christian, the son of a South-German captain of industry, traveling from house-party to house-party, mingling with the international set who are forever straying from one European capital to

another in the effort to amuse themselves. He
is everything which the folk of our day have
persuaded themselves they want most to be.
He is handsome, fearless, powerfully attractive to both men and women, immensely
wealthy, of noble manners, idolized by both his
parents; he has nothing at all to do save to pass
his days in entertaining himself. His friends
are very much occupied in finding him a mistress or a wife worthy of him, and only in the
person of Eva Sorel, a sort of Eleanora Duse
of the dance, do they find his equal. But there
is an element in Christian which begins to elude
his fashionable friends. There has always been
some sort of apartness, some mystical light,
resting upon him; it is perhaps this that has
made everybody love him; it now begins a
strange development. The death of a friend,
some conversations with a young Russian revo-
lutionist escaped from Siberia, the misfortune
of a lover of Eva's whom Christian had sought
to supplant, the sight of the defilement of a
girl by a band of half-drunken students, wakens in him a sympathy that begins to consume
him. Hitherto strong only in the external
graces, devoid entirely of the ability to penetrate into the lives of his fellows, he begins to

lose joy in his wealth, his luxury, his position. It becomes worthless to him; and something which he has never seen before becomes all-valuable. He begins to see everywhere, in everyone, almost impersonally, a thing that is not himself, not others, and yet himself and all men. It is *that* which he comes to love with the strange incandescency of a frigid man. It is that which he loves in all his fellows. It is that which he wants to have acknowledged.

Christian leaves Eva Sorel; he adopts a poor, rotting prostitute and settles in the slums of Berlin. There he encounters the woman with whom he falls in love. She is a young Jewish girl endowed with precisely the same quality of passionate universal love which has begun to develop in him. She, too, needs no objective power to be fulfilled; she has the secret of life in her. It is the human soul in her, the pilgrim soul, that Christian loves. Ruth is murdered by a perverted creature, a sort of Jack the Ripper; the old revenge of those degraded by existence on those to whom it is given to be holy, is revealed to Wahnschaffe. He knows the murderer, and goes to him. "Are you going to report me?" the ripper demands. Christian replies: "I am not going to report you. I do not even know whether you are really guilty of the deed you have done. But you must give me something. You have taken from me the most beautiful thing in the world. You have taken from me something that is so beautiful that it almost seems as though the world could not go on without it. Now you must give me something in its place.'' For the first time in his existence, Christian weeps. At first the man does not understand him. They speak together; they go about together. Christian shows no hatred, no condemnation of him. Then, because of Christian's utter humility, something takes place in the murderer's mind. A sudden light flares in him; he understands Christian. He goes away to give himself up to the police. He has given to Christian what Christian wanted of him, the acknowledgement of the reality of the human soul. Wahnschaffe disappears from Berlin; the novel dies away like a legend, a modern saga. The author tells us that at one time rumors reached his old friends that Christian had been seen in Ham during a catastrophe in the mines; at another, that he had appeared in the East End of London among the very poor; at a third, that he had been seen in the Chinese district of New York. Then he disappears for all time.

More than a brilliant vulgarization of the works of the great mystic Russian, *The World's Illusion,* however, is not. One likes, of course, certain elements of the story. It is a piece of virtuosic story telling; direct and rapid; and in many instances, truly touching. Yet, much as one would like to do so, and in spite of its skilful mechanics and invention, one cannot quite bring oneself to agree with those who have found in the work an independent and substantial achievement. No doubt Wassermann has written, in *The World's Illusion,* his most successful novel. Its superiority over *Das Gansemännchen,* which preceded it, is evident. Nevertheless, one finds it deficient in certain respects exactly as *Jean Christophe,* with which it has been compared, is deficient. Not that the work is an imitation of Dostoievsky, even though certain scenes toward the close of the second volume, principally those between Christian and the ripper, savor a little over-strongly of episodes in both *The Idiot* and *The Brothers Karamazov.* Wassermann is a practicing novelist with his proper theory of the novel, and his latest work has a distinct physiognomy. What one finds wanting in the novel is the realization of the author's idea, the establishment of a literary form symbolical of the author's emotion. Wassermann has not succeeded in embodying his theories. For him, of course, the art of fiction is entirely the art of creating living, sharply designed characters. Of no avail, he knows, is the creation of atmosphere, the elaborate descriptions and analyses of the naturalistic novelists. A character understood and loved by the author will create the necessary atmosphere about him, and no analysis or elaborate stage-setting can compensate for the weaknesses of an author unable to feel his protagonists as vivid wholes. Wassermann has written several essays, *Die Kunst der Erzählung, Der Literat als Psychologe,* in defense of his theories, and *The World Illusion,* better even than they, reveals how sincere is his concern with the technique of narrative, how unflagging his attempts to create objectivities in his fictions. He has not shrunk from creating, or seeking to create, characters upon a grandiose scale, and letting his story move entirely through them. He interjects descriptions and analyses very sparingly;

his action proceeds through a dry, direct narrative, and through fairly essentialized conversations.

But the task he has set himself is one somewhat too large for him. The types he has succeeded in showing us remain, after all, most of them, lay figures. Neither Christian nor Eva, Niels Heinrich nor Ruth Hoffman, his victim, Karen the prostitute nor Becker the revolutionary, takes possession of us with anything of the insistence of Lucien or Vautrin or Madame Marneffe, Raskolnikov or Katharina or Muichkin. If Crammon and Johanna are more real, if Amadeus Voss is one of the best studies of the Judas in all modern art, better even than that in *Savva* by Andreyev, Wassermann's successes do not quite make good the slight woodenness of his principal figures. What it is the author lacks, above all is a certain singleness of interest. He is very evidently torn between two horses: the one, his feeling about life and his experience of it; the other, a certain routine of story telling which makes him sacrifice his art in the effort of being perfectly effective and intriguing. That is, he is a man of two classes; and he falls, with all his genuine talent and observation, between

the stools of art and of best selling. In consequence, he begins with preconceptions of what
a good story well told is; begins perhaps with
a hard and fast plot, in which automatons run
predestined courses. His drama therefore
verges on melodrama; and some of his dynamic
characters go ahead on wooden legs. Moreover,
the last few hundred pages of *The World's
Illusion* are sliced up arbitrarily for the purpose of sustaining a hectic interest in the
denouement and supplying thrills. What most
clearly adumbrates Wassermann's characteristic duality of interest is the absence of any very
noteworthy word-sensations in his prose. And
even a certain intellectual power of observation
fails him at moments, and leaves him quite
cheap in his invention. For all his detail, his
attempt to render the *tempo* of the modern
world; his people who trail from hunting parties in Scotland to house-parties in Franconia,
from Petrograd to Paris, his fashionable Ger-
mans who quote Stefan Georg and chase
drinks of wine with drinks of champagne, ale,
whiskey, coffee, and again wine; his many little
pictures of the collapse of industrial civilization; for all this, he has not succeeded in
feeling directly the life of Europe before the

war. Both the fashionable world of the first volume and the underworld of the second are too much the upper and underworlds with which romantic popular fiction has been playing during the last decades.

Consequently, one is continually obliged to be indulgent with the author; to pretend to be accepting his rhinestones for fine diamonds; to accept his intention in the place of what he has actually given. Still, one finds oneself rejoiced that the book has been translated. If Wassermann is a popular novelist, at least one can read his work with a certain amount of amusement and satisfaction, which is more than one can do with the productions of popular Americans and Englishmen. Moreover, the spirit of it makes one glad. Here, we know, is testimony that somewhere there is a man who has learned something from the war; somewhere, a cubit has been added to the human stature. The race is attempting to compensate itself in some fashion for the harm it has done itself. And if one deems this evidence the great contribution of the work, one is attributing to it a virtue of indubitable size.

JENS PETER JACOBSEN

JENS PETER JACOBSEN

JACOBSEN is the seraph of Danish literature. Even in translation his prose sings
with frail unearthly fervor. Across scenes of
desire and of death, of yearning and of catastrophe, the tender melodiousness spreads a
soft and golden tone. The world lies mellow
in these novels like light caught on surfaces
of highly waxed old wood. *Marie Grubbe,*
"interiors" from out the courtly life of the
seventeenth century, is the work of a Vermeer
in words, and pearly as one of the canvases of
the magic Dutchman. And the semi-biograph-
ical *Niels Lyhne* is a poem of late summer
afternoon and sunset, suffused deeply with the
very breath of the hour. Images may lift the
prose into wild romantic flight; the soul may
speak to Niels in savage trumpet blasts; and
sprays of blossoming roses build castles and
vaulted choirs with their fat bloom. But vi-
brancy and power are both absent from the
tone. The springtide when it comes flooding
the valley where the anæmic northern woman

Niels' mother lies dying is honeyed and hurt-
less, soft and idyllic and caressing only; a drift
of naïve bright flowers, a sparkle of gliding
waters, a rain of soft delicious lights and
scents. And the vignettes of the damp, dreary
northern fall, and of the wet and endless
Baltic winter, are suffused equally with the
wistfulness and delicacy of sunset hue.

It lies, the wistfulness, in the tales themselves not less than in the carrying form.
They, too, have a "dying fall"; bring dreamy
and rich tenderness awash together; sing with
the bowing of the heart before the helpless-
ness of the feminine soul. *Marie Grubbe* figures the destiny of the passive creature
through the person of a patrician woman of
the court of Frederick the Third, dainty and
over-tense, filled with infinite capacity for passion and pain; and submitted helplessly to the
men to whom she gives herself; first the handsome faithless bastard; then the courtier weak
and sensitive like herself; last the groom who
takes her far from the life she has known into
poverty, and loves her and beats her because
he loves her, and then is brought back to her
cabin broken and dying. Through a protagonist of a different sex and through the atmos-

phere of a different century, *Niels Lyhne*
achieves much the same effect. For the exquisite reconstructions of the scenery and
spirit of the past there are substituted tiny
impressionistic paintings of the Danish countryside and of Copenhagen before the war of
1864. But the narrative sings the same painful
wonder over the destiny of the inactive in-
agressive being. The hero is the weary end of
an ancient line, a half poet of sensuous ineffectual cast. And all the characters in the novel,
Niels' mother like himself, Begum, Mrs. Boye,
Fennimore, Gerda, are dreamers, dainty and
lacking in power of the will. The mother
passes her girlhood in perpetual daydream,
tries to find a reality in marriage, and sinks
disappointed into her fantasies. Only during
the months when death is close upon her does
she taste of the living beauty for which she
pined all her days. Niels, apparently gifted
for creation, possessed of the capacity for feeling from which poetry is supposed to flow,
welling in exquisite and poignant emotions,
never achieves anything durable. Some inward fatigue weighs upon him. He cannot
successfully leave his dreams. Loves and a
marriage come to Niels. But life slips through

his fingers. His friends die or become estranged from him. After the death of his young wife and child he loses interest in living; and in the end perishes in the Schleswig war rich in ecstasy and suffering, and poor of some miracle which should have happened and filled his hands, and never came.

Jacobsen was faced with imminent death while working on these romances. Restless years in Copenhagen filled with inconclusive love affairs and much dissipation had eaten heavily into his small store of health; and he returned to his mother in the country under sentence from the doctors, and condemned to a bare régime. And in the dreamy beauty of his tales, he expressed the feeling of his own end which could not ever have been far from him those last years: *vita somnium breve;* existence full of rich and painful things, and yet unsubstantial as mist; destiny carrying him upon its silent rushing stream into known gray lands far from the comforting and familiar objects to which he would have clung. But it is not only the sign of an individual state of being which this impeccable hand set down. The resignation, the softness and dreamy melancholy of these tales is characteristic of

nineteenth century Denmark after the defeat
at the hands of Prussia; and characteristic at
the same time of a condition which transcended
by far the confines of the small Scandinavian
state. Want of some inner faith in life, some
power of momentum, was in the cultivated individuals the world through; and left them
static and directionless in a luxurious atmosphere. And sometimes, it is the whole north
of many centuries that speaks in this wistful
music. Unfriendly nature has ever tended to
produce folk rich in inner development, in
imagination and the power of feeling, and still
curiously incapable of laying aggressive hand
upon the moment. The blood rushes up, and
then hesitates near the surface; an immediate response and clearing does not come.
Devastating northern longing: the yearning
of the human being, cast into bitter climes, for
the warmth, the ease and carelessness of the
south and the sun, sucks life away. And yet,
no south and tropic heat can bring relaxation.
In Africa, fulfillment remains as distant as in
Scotland and Brandenburg and Denmark.
There is no giving in; and yearning, always.

These novels are part of general European
literature, too, through the influence exerted

by them. They have played a rôle in the development of the novel in countries other than
their own; in Germany, particularly. For just
as Jacobsen the lyric poet has come to stand
in something of the relation of a forerunner to
Stefan Georg, to Rainer Marie Rilke and
Hugo von Hofmannsthal, to the entire group
of German poets moving toward ever more
refined means of expression, so Jacobsen the
romancer has contributed to the defeat of the
naturalistic school of novel-writing in Teu-
tonic lands. With *Marie Grubbe,* with
Mogens and in particular with *Niels Lyhne,*
he helped exorcise Zola, and bring about a
recrudescence of the analytical novel. For
just and poetic translations are the rule in
Germany; and *Niels Lyhne,* little diminished
in the process of adaptation, appeared in
German at the moment when its particular
impulse was most living. It was the moment
when the reaction against the complete pre-
occupation with the composition of society
and complete neglect of the psychology of
the individual, of which Zola and his fol-
lowers all over the Continent had been so
guilty, had begun to gather head in artistic
circles. The century, it will be remembered,

had begun with transcendentalism, and seen
flourish a novel that mirrored and analyzed
almost exclusively the self. Indeed, for the
novelists of the romantic school, the world itself was but an emanation of the ego. But
with the rise of industrialism and the ascend-
ancy of its accompaniment, positivism, the
novel had swerved into the study of the forces
and conditions of nature and society to which
the individual is subjected. The self ceased
to interest exclusively, and diminished in importance for the novelist. In Balzac, the two
worlds, the subjective and the objective, are
still fairly well balanced. But with the arrival
of naturalism, the psychology of the individual was degraded to minor importance. In the
novels of Zola the characters are not very much
more than types—prostitutes, laborers,
peasants, artists, priests and others. The
world is conceived as having an existence entirely independent of the visions of the characters. Indeed, it is almost conceived as
having an existence entirely independent of
the vision of the novelist himself. To be sure,
Zola had defined the naturalistic novel as "nature viewed through a temperament." In
truth, however, his ideal was the scientific

document, the abstract and passionless narration of "facts." Had he been able, he would have created fictions approximating the deadly reports of social investigators. Luckily for the novel, Zola oftentimes failed of his goal. He was too much the rhapsode, the symphonist. The tediousness of complete impersonality has been attained only by his unique disciple, Pierre Hamp. Still, his theories, his pseudo-scientific attitude, continued to weigh upon the form. Before the visions of the novelists all over Europe there continued to float the *ignis fatuus* of the "experimental" romance, the scientific work.

Toward 1885, the individualistic reaction set in. The self was once more become the center, the principal matter, the object of analysis. The new psychological novel was born; Bourget introduced Stendhal anew to France; Maeterlinck translated Novalis; in Germany, folk ceased laughing at the romantic school. And if the pendulum did not swing back all the way to the ground of the romanticists, if novelists did not again conceive the world as an emanation of the ego, nevertheless, Zola's conception of a world independent of the vision of his characters, was entirely abandoned. The study of the external world as the mirror and revealer of the self, came into being. Henceforward, landscapes, inanimate nature, the objective world, were to be represented only because of what the characters felt toward them and because of the strata of their selves revealed in the transference.

And Jacobsen in *Niels Lyhne* gave the young German novelists of the nineties a perfectly realized example of a "subjective" novel. Of his two chief works, *Marie Grubbe* is perhaps the less "subjective"; it is more dramatic, and full of a color which is more of the century than of the heroine. Indeed, at moments it seems slightly derivative from the "interiors" of the Dutch painters. But *Niels Lyhne* pictures primarily the states of an individual soul, and with profound psychological insight records the development of a sensibility. It concerns itself almost exclusively with the inner life of its hero, with his feelings and fantasies and moods. The novelist lingers with greatest love over the moments of intense lyricism, when the soul of his man becomes an ecstatically vibrating organ. And though the drama stands clear, the lyrical states embody the story no less than the scenes of action. Moreover, the world of Niels is exclusively his own idea. The very quality of the hero and his mother come to us through the landscapes and descriptive pieces.

And throughout the post-naturalistic epoch of German prose, one feels the influence of this finely shaded painting of elusive mood. It is in Schnitzler, in Mann, in Voigt-Diedrichs. If their prose has remained less diapred and melodious, and their novel-writing more documentary, they nevertheless follow on many paths trampled by Jacobsen. The dreamy young Viennese of Schnitzler, responsive to scarcely another interest than love; Tonio Kröger and Hanno Buddenbrook of Mann, what are they but younger brethren of Niels Lyhne? More recently, another figure has joined the cohort of brothers. It is that of Malte Laurids Brigge, of Rilke; Niels Lyhne once again; but become more sinisterly enervate and neurotic.

Possibly, for us, *Marie Grubbe* will prove more lastingly attractive. We have had the benefit of the form of *Niels Lyhne,* and the stuff of the earlier book is a little more solid. Jacobsen was a dying man when he wrote the history of the nineteenth century dreamer,

Frühgereift und zart und traurig; and his illness seems in one or two instances to have dimmed his artistic vision. The book smells a trifle overmuch of lavender. The latter chapters, which deal with the maturity of the hero, are somewhat thinner than the earlier ones recounting his boyhood and adolescence. Unable to live himself out because of his consuming malady, Jacobsen was doubtlessly unwilling to face the maturity of his character with the same intensity with which he faced his youth; and less richly stocked with material for the painting of the man's years. Very little is said of the wedlock of Niels and his girl-wife. And although the picture of Niels' encounter with his young aunt in the darkened, rose-scented room; of his farewell to Erik; and of Fennimore's revery in the warm chamber while she waits for her lover stand clear in one's memory as beautifully achieved things, the novelist has expended the treasures of his lyricism most lavishly on the scenes of death which are too frequent, and nearly cloying. The novel is overful of premature deaths. Practically each one of the principal characters meets an untimely end. Niels' father and mother die in early middle life. Edele, Erik, Gerda, Niels himself, perish in their youth. It is a little as though Jacobsen, aware of his own swiftly approaching extinction, and overcome by the pathos of his existence, had unconsciously desired to insist upon, and bring forcibly home to his readers, the sadness of a lot like his own.

And still, there is little to choose between the two little masterpieces. One shuts both books with the satisfaction which comes from having encountered beautifully accomplished work. With somewhat less of appetite, less of volume and flow than his contemporaries in France and Russia had, Jacobsen nevertheless achieved almost perfectly what he set out to do, and produced rich things with unforgetable suave and singing surfaces. We return to them. For they were made with the wisdom of the violet and the pine: and both plants are content to remain themselves.

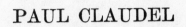

PAUL CLAUDEL

PAUL CLAUDEL

BY the largeness of his gesture Paul Claudel immediately set himself apart both from the Catholic poets and the other literary figures of his time. Other religious poets had gained the ear of France during those last years before the war, and were beginning to gain the ear of the world as well. But by the side of this grave and rapt and apostolic approach the Virgilian piety of Francis Jammes grew a little pale, the mystic sociology of Charles Péguy got a suspicion of Tolstoy and holy-water. Claudel brought with him the vast spatial feeling of a passionate and tragical apprehension of life. Something of the air of the Gothic world itself, with its anxiety, its anguish, and abundant fervor, returned in his free and clamant verse. Once more, the accents of a soul in intense and bloody struggle with its God were to be heard, and they were good to hear in the house of letters.

It was an art of bold rough strokes brought by Claudel. It was an art of large pierc-

ing human images drawn from daily life and
ships and machinery, and of a violent and exalted style formed on the Greek and Hebrew
poets and sown with foreign and technical
terms which it had taken up into itself. It was
an art all mouth, straining to hold the utterance close to the fluid form which it had taken
when it left the burning fountain of the soul,
and careless of accepted euphony and measure. Expression, that was what it sought: the
bark, the shriek, the coo of the being seated
in the human frame down where there are no
words, and gestures, beats, starts and rhythms
only exist. With pride it gave itself as product of that

> fonction double et réciproque
> Par laquelle l'homme absorbe la vie, et restitue
> dans l'act suprême de l'expiration
> Une parole intelligible.

By word Claudel pointed to Rimbaud as his
source and his tradition. But even more than
the pledge of word, the physiognomy of this
verse spewed out in a sort of sublime intoxication, pointed to roots in the emotional, mystical, irrational tradition of French poetry.

Periodically French genius shifts from
search for God through reason to search for

God through faith, from the thought of Paris
to the thought of Chartres. After Voltaire
there came Chateaubriand; after Anatole
France there came the movement of which
Claudel is a great integral part. Without pre-
sumption Claudel laid the scene of several of
his dramas in that triangle of earth lying between the cathedrals of Rheims, Soissons and
Laon. Physically he sprang from that
ground; spiritually also; and the presence
above him of the three Gothic nurses conditions the struggle of his soul. Hence, precisely as he opposed to the accepted intellectual
logic of academic France an inner emotional
logic, so he opposed to the emotional guarded-
ness, the slightly overwise precaution of Voltaire and Renan and Anatole France the passionateness, the tribulation, the daringness of
his own nature. Astute man of affairs, consul
in Boston and New York, Tientsin and Fou-
chow, Frankfort and Hamburg; an authority
on the economic situation in China, shortly to
become minister to Brazil and ambassador to
Japan, he came to make us hear once more that
life lies in the search for beatitude. There was
but one grand theme for him: the knowledge
of God. It was his subject in ode and drama.

One had to go back to Æschylus to find another dramatist so preoccupied. The man's life had been comprised in that search. As if to make bodily attestation that *la vision de dieu engendre la vie eternelle,* he went into the exile of distant consulates, the Frenchman's bitter exile, to seek the face of his fate. The dramas he composed during those twenty years of self-imposed banishment bear witness to the singleness of a purpose. All the protagonists are searchers for God, and all are crucified. Mesa in *Partage du Midi;* Sygne de Coûfontaine in *L'Otage;* the Emperor in *Le Repos du Septième Jour,* all are broken by the revelation when it comes.

The knowledge of God was ever associated in the mind of Claudel both with worldly loss, outcast state and bitter renunciation, and supreme abiding bliss. In the East, the consul must have seen many human beings cast out from their families and villages because of disease, and condemned to death in life, and their fate seemed to him, it appears, little different from that of individuals chosen for the kiss and knowledge and sight of God. And still, he tells us again and again that all that tears us from love and hope of happiness here on earth, brings us nearer to the one great happiness, the one great love. The problem was posed for the first time in Claudel's earliest drama, and his latest did not let it go. There, in the first version of *Tête d'Or* written in 1889, he tried to give the picture of a humanity striving to possess the earth and the supreme values at once, and coming despairingly against the black wall of death. The protagonist is the superman as he might have appeared to the young French generation of thirty-five years since; the drama expressed the failure and burial of a great Pagan hope. And the overwhelming sense of mortality, the deep and abiding grief over a world that cannot be held, which spoke in grandiose and pathetic accents from out this overture of a career, remained everpresent in the work of Claudel. But in the twenty years that elapsed between the composition of *Tête d'Or* and the gorgeous *L'Annonce fait à Marie,* the vision became suffused with a light of joyous resignation. To all the persons of this mystery the terrible stigmata comes. It comes to Violaine, the innocent girl smitten by leprosy, and cast out from all human ties until "only the soul lives in the human body." It comes to her two lovers, neither of whom may possess her here upon the earth. It comes to the old man Anne Vercors who sets out from home and surfeit of earth on a lonely pilgrimage toward the Lord of the Universe. But over them all, as over the leper woman in the scene of the miracle, the Heavens open. For Death and God are one.

> Is the object of life only to live? Will the feet of God's children be fastened to this wretched earth?

And then the answer comes:

> It is not to live, but to die, and not to hew the cross, but to mount upon it, and give all that we have, laughing!
> There is joy, there is freedom, there is grace, there is eternal youth.

A certain suspicion of sadism was not to be banished from one's mind while reading these plays. Like so much contemporary "mysticism," they seemed an attempt to mint spiritual values from ugly outlawed desires. Nevertheless, for the great measure of genuine power and sincerity and lyricism contained in them one accepted the ounce of chaff with the pound of wheat. But it is not as facile a matter accepting Claudel's recent works. These latter poems and plays want the largeness and immediacy of expression which the older ones had; and the disagreeable Claudelian elements have become exaggerated in them. This is particularly true of the dogmatic element. The aristocratic, Catholic and royalist ideas of the earlier work constitute an integral portion of the structures in which they occur, for the reason that they constituted an integral portion of the poet's individuality and therefore of his vision of things. But in the later works the aristocratic, royalist and Catholic elements have become part of a thesis which the poet has deliberately set out to teach. Claudel has become official. He prays he may not be damned with Hugo and Michelet and Renan; anathemizes the German heresiarchs Goethe and Kant and Nietzsche and *leur père à tous, l'apostate Martin Luther, qui est avec le diable!* It would seem the poet went to confession too often; and was permitting certain black personages not primarily interested in the art of the poet to use him for their own pious ends. One finds oneself automatically adding Claudel to the list of intelligences invalided by the reaction of war and after-war.

He will live, therefore, by the might of the works written while he was still first the poet and second the official and good Catholic. For his word, whatever his intention, went out beyond official boundaries. It was not after all to war upon heretics and infidels, Turks and Jews, in the theological sense, that he came. It was rather more to force again upon the world the necessity of a faith in life; to remind those people who, in the words of Blake, "are not capable of a firm persuasion of anything" that without genuine conviction life is impossible. He came to return to us the light that existence upon this earth is a pilgrimage in search of some great fulfillment of the soul. With a superb gesture he brushed from his own consciousness all that might lead him away from this great knowledge; and that gesture is itself an abiding glory.

JOHANNES V. JENSEN

JOHANNES V. JENSEN

ON a hotel-register Johannes V. Jensen
once inscribed himself "traveling sales-
man for anthropological goods." Globe-trotting and the study of mankind indeed have
been united by the Danish author into a single
act. Voyages to Birubunga and Pekin, Chicago
and Singapore; profane knowledge of Seville
and Paris have given plasticity to ideas of
the physical and mental development of the
human being. Speculation on the origin and
customs of races has thrown colored light on
coasts and forests and cities seen, and made an
intellectual adventure of steamship and railway travel.—Cloudbursts drench the Indian
ocean; the day is torrid under the sun; rain
sweeps again; night presses against him like
the belly of an animal, and he imagines the
earth of the mezozoic period. Crete with its
arid rocky sides and misted mountaintops recalls characteristics of its culture and suggests
bases for its legendary rôle. The bedside lamp
in a Berlin hotel-room carries his fancy to the

wheel generative of the electric current: he perceives the vast modern towns built about the wheels as bodies are built around hearts, and dependent for life on the revolutions of the metal things. Sitting on the glass-enclosed steamer-chair deck of a liner in winter sunshine, he picks apart in his mind the components of the giant machine transporting him, and glimpses like a bannered history the long development behind each. It seems he is one of the men who have gotten the best excitements the rapid modern means of communication have to give. Not Kipling nor Morand have gotten finer pleasures from them; Jensen's volumes sparkle with the fruits of a mind taken sightseeing.

The works in which he has sought to give form to his experiences fall into two general classes. Both ambitiously set out to give the picture, the proportions and direction of life as we understand it in our day; but the one seeks to achieve it through direct description, and the other through the medium of primitive myth. In the first, which comprises the volumes of essays and stories translated out of the Danish under the titles *The New World, Our Age, The World is Deep, Exotic Tales,*

and the two early thrillers *Madame D'Ora*
and *The Wheel,* the subject is the modern
scene. Jensen is himself the protagonist,
in several instances, and the matter is playfully autobiographical. In the late nineties,
he tells us, fresh from the university, he
was scribbling dime novels and literary re-
views in Copenhagen. And there came over
him a hatred for himself, and for a world "for
which he was neither bad nor vulgar enough."
"Sick with the northern sickness, incurable
longing," he tramped and shipped about the
globe. "I was nervous, quivering like a delirious man. The pity of it all was that alco-
holism hadn't made me so. Drink, at least,
quiets one. The trouble with me was that I
was inactively self-conscious, conscious of myself in every nerve, the victim of an unbridled
imagination." That was his Gothic labora-
tory, and pilgrimage took him out of it. It
showed him his time had a beauty. He was
among the first to perceive that we are living
in a sort of Renaissance. All great ages, Jensen knew, have sought either to turn human
energy from the world, or restore it fully to it.
The Christianizing centuries were moved by
the first of these tendencies. The Renaissance,

the Reformation and the French Revolution
sought to bring human energy back to the
earth. But the three great attempts at resto-
ration were unsuccessful. The impulse of the
humanistic revival went into the heaping up
of erudition for its own sake, and ended as
philology in the library. If Luther in Germany did emancipate, it was merely in order
to bind again with other bonds. The revolution attempted to transform the human being
into an idea. Not so our own day. It alone
has rid itself of all theories and conceptions
which divert man from his earthly existence.
It alone has come again to the consciousness,
characteristic of the youth of races, of the self-
sufficiency of existence, the supreme importance of life itself. The stream of the libido
has returned from theories, from hopes of
extra-mundane heavens, to the one reality, the
struggle with nature. With the re-employ-
ment of man's forces, the dreams that have
been humanity's since the caveman in his cavern dreamt of flying, have begun to be realized.
Other ages dreamt too of power over nature
and defiance of natural laws; but they had
been content to find satisfaction in myths, and
in realizing their wishes in the shape of gods.

Ours has begun turning the stuff of dreams
into actuality. The earth is young again; and
Jensen, gazing out over Paris, pitied Nietzsche,
who had lived into himself instead of out "into
a world that was far better than he."

The trilogy *The Long Journey* illustrates
Jensen's second form. In these "myths," he
has attempted to give his poetic picture of
life through a union of anthropological theory
with the atmosphere, lyricism and innocence
of the ancient sagas. Each of the sections of
Fire and Ice, the first volume, shows primitive humanity at some crisis of its career; but
in each of these little romances Jensen has
symbolized the life of every man who breaks
with the past, returns to the giant realities,
and is created anew out of his very struggle
with nature for his livelihood. The section
called *Ice,* perhaps the most successful of
all, in particular fables the birth of Jensen's
own Gothic race. The scene is laid in prehis-
toric times when the glacier came down over
Scandinavia and overwhelmed the tropical
forests which once had flourished there. Carl,
the protagonist, is the first anarchist. Driven
from his tribe which is flying south before
hardship and winter, he turns north and com-

bats the cold. In the bitter struggle for life he adapts himself to a new environment. Human will is born. Carl maintains his life. He learns to make fire. On an island amid the glacier he rears sons and daughters. And, one night in his cave, the First Man dreams. First, he seems to be swimming through a tropical sea. The other animals avoid him in fear; and he rises toward a steaming shore. Then, he is in a mighty city. It is Chicago, alive with machinery and noise and the ferocity of the interhuman combat for existence. And last, Carl dreams of a forest of living trees, rocks of bone, and earth of breathing flesh. Over it floats "the sign of eternal resurgence." And in his cave, the First Man dies.

Another romance, not included in the English edition, and called *The Ship* sings the day of a race that had the power to destroy life and create it anew. It tells the story of the Danes who conquered Normandy and England; and again the story is but a symbol for a certain realistic principle Jensen feels in our own time. One episode might stand the epitome of his idea. A band of famished lads in search of food have broken into a Norse temple. "For a moment they stood rooted. In the glow of their torches, the Gods, misshapen figures covered with crusts of dried blood, seemed to step out of the blackness and stand staring at them. And for an instant, the young marauders were aghast. It was so silent there. The dread Gods appeared to be gazing at them from all parts of their forms. But at last Germund came to himself. Shaking the sparks from his torch, he stepped forward and boldly cried, 'Is any corn hidden here?'"

All Jensen's ideas are instantaneous flashing pictures seen from the bridges of ships and platforms of moving trains. Even in Denmark, at his worktable, he is globe-trotting. Hence, scarcely a one of them possesses the solidity born of patient, well-sustained scrutiny. It is entirely in their suggestiveness that their charm and value lie. The man himself has not quite the metaphysical, penetrative power of the artist and scientist of the premier water. His background of anthropological study is not wide, and certain of his impressions reveal themselves a little superficial and sensational. Particularly when writing about America is he too much the dreamer and the sentimentalist. "What stories of mythological wonders can compare with the narration of the life that goes on in America to-day" he told us a little ante-Cody, ante-dada and ante-Josephson; and enlarged on the romance of our existence, the poetry of big business, the young sound strength of it all. Well, it may be true that the machines are proof of the fact that man's imagination and power, instead of wandering off into interstellar space in the shape of theories and systems, has returned to the world as energy; and that beauty inevitably follows power and results from an economy of means based upon practicality. But to us here in the land of the "new beauty," it appears that Jensen, like some of his epigones, has in one instance at least mistaken style for significance, and permitted himself to believe a style without content equivalent to culture.

Besides, his myths are not thorough objectivities. The heroes are always identical; only their names and external adventures are differentiated. One, brings fire from the mountain and is Prometheus; another, survives winter on the glaciers and is Odin; a third, invents the wheel and is Thor. But in each case it is

the same man who is figured: the big blond
genius as he appears to a slightly infantile
imagination. *The Cimbrians* recalls Henty
not infrequently. Episodes in *Columbus*
dealing with the conquest of Mexico by Cortez
verge on cheapness. As a poetical interpretation of this hideous chapter of history they
are by no means as respectable as another
imaginative work recently come out of the
north of Europe: the *Montezuma* of Ger-
hardt Hauptmann.

It may be that absence of profundity is
merely the inevitable shadow of Jensen's positive gift, and that his particular quality of
impressionability and imaginative quickness
could not have existed in a system capable of
slower, steadier penetration. In any case, the
man has turned his superficiality to best account. He has promenaded his epidermis, and
registered the sharp and vivid contrasts, the
novel sights and sounds and smells to which
it has responded. More poetical than Kipling,
less dry than Conrad often is, he stands eminent for his descriptions of exotic and pre-
historic landscapes; chapters in *Fire and
Ice* are very poems in prose. *The World is
Deep* and *Exotic Tales,* profane adventures

of an anthropologist in Sumatra, Seville,
Montmartre, blend sophistication piquantly
with rabelaisian gusto. And men who come
with the vision of the proportions and beauty
of a day come bringing an impulse to freedom.

MR. NOCK

MR. NOCK

WE ought to be jubilant, we in America who are in need of learning. It appears that we are about to be taught. There is someone come who says he knows where he can procure us "sound spiritual guidance." We are also to be given the opportunity of becoming great artists. For the sound spiritual guides are going to "set before us the great examples of classic work," to "stimulate our feelings for great classic work," and give us "assurance that the effect of this great classic work can be reproduced and assist us in reproducing it." The years of wandering in the wilderness are past for us. Canaan is but over the next hillock. All that any one of us, large or small, will have to do to be produced beautifully will be to listen to the words our guides are going to speak, and it will be given us to be, not the equals of the great masters, but their very selves.

Ezra Pound, for instance, if he should so

desire, can become Dante. For here is one come who says he knows where there are those who will not only be able to furnish him with ample assurance that "the effect" of the Divine Comedy can be reproduced, but will assist him in reproducing it. Sherwood Anderson, should he weary of himself, can be Dostoievsky. He has but to sit attentive, and permit himself to be helped. Marsden Hartley can paint the pictures of Greco. Nothing will be easier for him. Carl Sandburg can do a combination of the elder and the younger Eddas, with the Gilgamesh epic thrown in. T. S. Eliot can become Aristotle: is there not arisen among us one who knows where all can learn to reproduce the effect of the Poetics? And Van Wyck Brooks can be Lessing, Waldo Frank can be Balzac, and William Carlos Williams, Villon; and into Georgia O'Keeffe there can descend the gigantic brushmanship of Rubens. Let none be falsely modest. Let none hesitate for fear he is asking overmuch. There are those who can show us how to emulate the classic masters.

Have we not the word of Albert Jay Nock for it? For it is Mr. Nock who knows where he can find us the "sound spiritual guidance" we so deplorably lack. It is he who knows where there are those who can "set before us the great examples of classic work" and so forth. To be sure, our benefactor has not made it quite clear who is to be benefited. He refers to "the younger generation," a rather vague term, since a new generation is produced in America every four or five years. In one spot, it is quite definitely the youth of the age of Gilbert Seldes and John Farrar to whom he refers. But in another, he says that it is "the youth which is putting up some kind of struggle, however ineffectual, toward the things of the spirit" that is to be soundly guided; and who is there who is reading a little, thinking a little, working a little, who may not be legitimately said to be putting up, however ineffectually, "some kind of a struggle toward the things of the spirit"? And in a third, the reference is to every one whom no critic "has sought to animate and enthuse by continually holding up before him great examples of his art, *and showing him specifically how he might emulate them,*" which tacitly includes every worker now living in the United States and in

the remainder of the world. Hence, one seems
justified in assuming that the younger generation which is to be benefited includes all
men who are in need of learning, whether they
know they are or not. There is no one of us
who ought not be jubilant.

The identity of our spiritual guides Mr.
Nock has as yet not seen fit to reveal. He
would mention their names, he says of these
his future critics, were it not a little invidious
to do so. We are, however, given complete
assurance that he knows where his redeemers
live, and that they form part of Mr. Nock's
own "generation." But of the identity of this
generation there is little said. True, there is
a reference to "my unpopular time of life."
But men of the age of sixty years, if that is
what Mr. Nock means, are not invariably unpopular with the "young." Both George
Santayana and Alfred Stieglitz are men of
sixty years of intense existence, and they are
men to whom most of us look up with admiration, and accept as guides.

The generation of Mr. Nock, is then, implic-
itly, the generation of those whose education
is completed, who have nothing more to learn,

and who can now with ease do for those less
fortunate than themselves what "Goethe and
Arnold and Sainte-Beuve did." The net total
of general culture—has tended to civilize them.
They have had, Mr. Nock admits for them, the
benefit of a certain amount of sound current
criticism;—"Saint-Beuve, Ruskin, Arnold
and Wordsworth, Goethe and Niebuhr,
Scherer, Renan, Emerson and Thoreau," it appears, "took them by the hand, gained their
confidence, sought to animate and enthuse them
by holding up before them the great examples
of their art, and showed them specifically how
they might emulate them."

Besides, there were great spiritual movements just before their time on the Continent
and in England, and they felt their backwash
and were energized by them. It seems, however, that some of these ineffable gifts were
misused, though, as Mr. Nock hastens to add,
not from lack of light or leading. It seems
that, for their successors, they "have chosen
to organize, actually to institutionalize, the
neglect of the things of the spirit, the disparagement of culture, the discouragement of
a free and disinterested play of thought, the
repression of the instinct of beauty and amen-

ity." For forty years, the tendency of all popular instruction provided by them in school, college and university "has been steadily against formative knowledge and in favour of a mere instrumental knowledge. A corresponding intention has animated every practical enterprise in which they have invited youth to participate.—To justify themselves, and give their procedure the weight and dignity of a philosophical codification, they have developed the doctrine of pragmatism."

Certain of these facts, descriptive of the past careers of the men who are to render us sound spiritual guidance, appear somewhat doubtful and strange qualifications for their new dignities. But they seem to satisfy Mr. Nock, who after all is the arbiter of such matters, having through the fortunate conditions obtaining at the time of his birth learnt, he assures us, "to give consideration to what Aristotle calls 'the determination of the judicious' in forming his own judgments."

It is to Mr. J. E. Spingarn we ought by right to be grateful for this ineffable boon that is about to descend on us. For it is he, "freest of amateurs, patron of esthetic radicalism," as Brooks has called him, who has, quite in-

advertently, it is true, procured it for us.
In a manifesto published in *The Freeman*
and entitled *The Younger Generation,* he
protested against those "who think that the
fragile and ephemeral moment of physical
youth is everything, that it is not merely the
whole of reality but the sole test of excellence."
"What shall we say" his manifesto continues
"of the fashionable theory of our day that all
art and all wisdom are the products of physical youth, that nothing is good unless men now
young have done it or like it, that everything
in the world is bad because it is the product
of elder statesmen or old artists, and that
therefore the test of ideas is not truth or the
test of art, excellence, but the only test for both
is 'modernity'?"

Unfortunately, in his very just protest
against the *morbus gallicus,*—for this sort
of reasoning is largely a product of French
literary life, and Louis Aragon and his group
have but lately made a particularly repulsive
restatement of something which has been on
the lips of several generations of French writers bent on slaying their fathers,—Mr. Spingarn poured out the baby with the bath. For he
left it to be gathered that all those, like Mac-

beth and his lady, "but young in deed" practice this vicious sort of log-rolling; whereas
in truth it is only a small and unimportant
group of the younger writers of America who
are really guilty. Because one immature
young editor devotes his magazine to puffing
every youngling who takes up the pen, particularly if that youngling happens to be a
product of the educational systems of Yale and
Princeton, was it fair of Mr. Spingarn to make
every one at present physically youthful, stand
in pillory? Was it at all just to hold an entire
group responsible for the indiscretion of a
couple of other editors of American magazines
published abroad? Besides, is it invariably
youth which sees in the fragile and ephemeral
state of youthfulness the great blessing? Is
it not as oftentimes those who are themselves
no longer in the April of life, who perceive
therein the supreme virtue?

And there is a growing band of writers,
physically young, who do not open their columns, if columns to open they do possess, alternately to toutings of the fledglings and of more
mature spirits of the genus of Edna Ferber.
There is this growing band for whom the test
of ideas is their truthfulness and the test of

art its excellence, and not the fact whether
ideas or art were produced today or six hundred years since. It is not its "modernity"
that caused T. S. Eliot to write his essay on
the metric of Pound. For "modernity" can
have no value for one who steeps himself of
will in the Elizabethans, and devotes his first
critical volume largely to examinations of
their poetry. It is not its "modernity" that
has made Pound unflaggingly acclaim the writing of James Joyce; for no more than for
Eliot can "modernity" be of value for one
who has won himself a sort of immortality
as the transmitter of old English, old French,
old Chinese poems; and whose latest volume
contains noteworthy interpretations of the
dry, caustic, Beotian spirit of Propertius.
It was certainly not his contemporaneity to
Randolph Bourne that produced in Van Wyck
Brooks the beautiful memorial to that poor
great soldier of liberty; nor is it synchrony
which makes Edmund Wilson write of Joyce
and Hemingway almost as poetically as he
writes of Virgil.

Has it indeed been anything more than the
standard of the truthfulness of ideas and the
excellence of art, that has made these writers

praise a work, whether or not it was produced yesterday or six hundred years ago? And if certain of the band of new critics are found more often praising the excellent work done in their own day than that done in the past, is it not rather because they love Dante more than because they love Dante less? Can one really understand the great man of the past and at the same time fail to perceive in the geniuses about one (genius inevitably unrecognized and struggling) some, no matter how small a quantity, of the same substance that moved in the giants of other days? It scarcely seems one can. No doubt, there may be men who appear to understand the great reliques of the past and still remain entirely unmoved by what is going on in their own hour. But it seems likely that the knowledge of such is merely the knowledge of the letter. It is certainly not the understanding of the spirit. For it is the nature of the spirit that it is recognizable under most divergent appearances. And recognition of it, like charity, always begins at home.

But it is precisely for his failure to make the obligatory distinctions between those physically young and those callow before mov-

ing onward to his praise of the idealism of
Croce and Gentile, that we ought heartily to
thank Mr. Spingarn. Because of it, a newspaper of large circulation and a small character mistook his article for an onslaught on
all those young in years who were poeticizing,
novelizing, criticizing, and used the opportunity to fill up its editorial columns with falsetto hurrahs over what it called "the passing
of the epidemic of infantile paralysis, which
has afflicted American literature"; and because of the newspaper editorial, Mr. Nock
issued his now justly famous call and ushered
in the present age of old men. Of the editorial itself, little need be said. It is the sympathetic repercussion of this newspaper wind
in the consciousness of the editor of a self-
styled radical weekly that remains interesting.

Mr. Nock, in his *Reviewer's Notebook,* found
the editorial "a strange production, malevolent and unscrupulous in temper, and yet in
every point of fact but one, whether stated
or implied—wholly sound"; the ability to find
something "strange, malevolent and unscrupulous in temper," "wholly sound in point of
fact, with one exception, whether stated or
implied" being vouchsafed him, we are to un-

derstand, it seems, by the Aristotelian discipline to which he submitted himself in his youth. He agreed that the young poets, critics and novelists are giving a sorry account of themselves. Although he himself could never make up his mind that "our youth is as bad as all this"—"headstrong, adventurous, unsuggestible, slow to see when it is making a fool of itself"—still, it may be. His sole point of difference with the editorial was, it seems, that the young were not originally damned, but the "victims of circumstance." He found repulsive, taunts against those upon whom misdirection and frustration had had full sway. "The intellectual and artistic flappers" might be as stupid and silly as one pleases, but was it not rather a marvel of the uncovenanted mercies of Providence that they were not ten times as stupid and silly?

For, it seems that the elder generation has not shared with the younger the immense advantages it itself enjoyed early in life. The elder generation—had had the encouragement to do better. In its youth, the net total of culture tended to civilize it; great spiritual movements energized it. However, for some reason or other, the elder generation has strin-

gently renounced and disparaged spiritual
elements. Therefore, concluded Mr. Nock, let
the older generation get away from undue pre-
occupation with the establishment of stark
theory and principle, let it "cease to regard
the creative artist as—a preacher's congre-
gation; and come to regard him as a fellow
striver, fellow worker, whose desires and aspi-
rations largely correspond with its own."
There are men who could do it admirably if
only they saw fit. They could, moreover, take
the next step in criticism, showing the relation of every activity of the human spirit with
the economic system under which it is practiced. At least—"youth would then have its
free choice of taking or rejecting a sound spiritual guidance."

And still, why is it that we who need to
learn, with all this apparent good reason for
jubilation, do not rejoice greatly? Why is it
that instead of arising as a single man and in-
toning the chorale *Es ist das Heil uns kom-
men her*, we find ourselves with difficulty
suppressing our mirth? One hears some prot-
estations; one hears a great deal more of half-
smothered laughter. Certainly, if we laugh,
it is not for the reason, that any of us is pre-

pared to reject real assistance were it to be offered us; much as the healthiness that knows no fat sweeter than that which sticks to its own bones might make us reject an offer to assist us in becoming a replica of a man dead, a replica even of the highest poet.

If then we smile, we who need so badly to learn, it is because, weak and ignorant as we are, we are not quite so simple as to mistake a confession of moral bankruptcy when it is made. By his own words, this man and those with whom he chooses to associate himself are attained of ghastly failure. By his own words, they are attained of treason to the things of the spirit. Sainte-Beuve, Ruskin, Arnold and Wordsworth, Goethe and Niebuhr, Scherer, Emerson, Renan and Thoreau, had done something for them, we are told; but we are also told that "for their successors, they chose to organize, actually to institutionalize, the neglect of those things, the disparagement of culture, the discouragement of a free and disinterested play of thought, the repression of the instinct of beauty and amenity." Having seen the light, they still played the Judas. Whatever we in our ignorance have done, certainly nothing as pitiable can, even by our greatest denigrators, be charged against us. And still, these very men are to provide others with "spiritual guidance"! What insolence. The self-confessed betrayers of a public trust pretending that it is they alone can manage a vast public utility!

But they do themselves—Mr. Nock and his "generation"—too much honor even in posing as great betrayers. They never were in the position to be grandly treasonable. They never perceived the light. For there is no receiving unaccompanied by a corresponding giving, and by their own mouths they prove they have not given. Had they really taken; had they really seen Goethe and Ruskin and Matthew Arnold plain, they could never have "done nothing to maintain and strengthen the tendencies" they pretend were imparted to them. They could never have been "steadily against formative knowledge and in favor of mere instrumental knowledge." They would have returned into the world, no matter what activity they found themselves engaged in, the light which they had drawn from its great minds.

No doubt at all, they knew the names of these great worthies. But Van Wyck Brooks has

taught us to see that all through the course
of American history, men have read in books
without acquiring practical knowledge; that
because of a split, characteristic of an entire
civilization, ideas existed without any relation
to practical living, and heads floated severed
of bodies. And it is precisely because of this
split that Mr. Nock and his "generation"
never understood clearly what it was they were
reading. He himself proves it. For though
he thinks he knows what the New Testament
signified by the word "krisis," he has never
understood the New Testament; otherwise, he
would not be selfrighteous and indulge in
pharisaical self-congratulations on his superior education.

And so they have little to give that is worth
giving. The veritable critic does not have
to be summoned, Cincinnatus-like, from the
plow. Your true-born critic, your Sainte-
Beuve, will submit himself to rigorous examinations of his conscience; but he will scarcely
ever cease from criticizing. The process end-
lessly engages his brain. He can scarce be
conscious without criticizing. Sooner or later,
he must burst into speech. For crystallizations are continually taking place in his mind,

because of the books he reads, the people he
meets, the talk he hears, the landscapes he sees.
Self-knowledge commences in him through
knowledge of some other thing, generally some
other work of art. It moves inward from
without; he begins with the examination of
the processes of another man and ends with
the realization that he has taken a step beyond
his old self. But Mr. Nock's critics do not
exist. For, were they truly critics, they would
not have had to wait upon his summons. They
are indeed, these men of his "generation," we
suspect strongly, figments of his fantasy.
They are projections of himself.

He himself, while this absurd pretentiousness has him in its grip, cannot assist in any
material way those who are seeking to create.
By the words of his article he demonstrates
that he has neither an understanding of the
creative nor the critical processes, if two
indeed they are. For he implies that creation
is the attempt to reproduce the effect of other
works, and that the function of criticism is to
assure the creator that such reproductions can
be made, and to assist him in making them.

Nor is he really interested in the thing before him, the young for whose welfare he pre-

tends to be so solicitous, save insomuch as
they might furnish a background which would
becomingly set him off. There can be no doubt
that the center of Mr. Nock's interest lies in
himself in the character of a sage "during the
few years before him" remorsefully but mag-
nificently illuminating benighted youth. For
there is not a word that he has written that
reveals that he has taken the smallest trouble
to scan the visages of those whose interest, he
declares, lies so close to his heart. He accepts
his phraseology from a newspaper editorialist
whose great complaint is that owing to the success of so many young novelists and critics
"those who were not young had to ape the
young."

He accepts his phraseology, then, from the
mouthpiece of gross time-servers, and adds not
a single expression that is applicable to even
one of as many divergent types of mind as
are represented by F. Scott Fitzgerald and
E. E. Cummings, by Louis Untermeyer and
Wallace Stevens. He is not even "up" on the
past of this youth. He speaks of a "next step
in criticism—showing the relation of every
activity of the human spirit—to the economic
system under which it is practiced," when it

was precisely that sort of criticism that was organized for the United States by Brooks in *America's Coming-Of-Age:* brilliantly developed by Bourne, Frank and several others, and is to-day undergoing assault from some of the younger writers.

Hence, we who need teaching have never been in the least deceived of the motive that has procured us this attempt at patronage. We have never been in the least deceived of the cause that has gained us this and deprived us of the veritable assistance which might have been rendered us by Mr. Nock, and which is indeed being rendered us by every one who is diligently seeking education, whether he be fifteen, fifty-five or ninety years of age, and whether or no he occupy himself with our immediate problems. We have not for a moment failed to recognize that Mr. Nock is not of the class of those who know they do not know, the class from which all real teachers, Socrates and every other, have been recruited, the class of those who create the intellectual situation necessary to the growth of art. The real teacher is always he who is the best of pupils; who never graduates himself from the company of those who need to learn; and who

is continually seeking wherever he can find
them better, clearer, finer, solutions for the
problems with which life persistently con-
fronts him. The real teacher is the man who
learns with men; the man who might write
over every book of his the superscription
placed by Arnold Schoenberg on his *Har-
monielehre—Dieses Buch habe ich von meinen
Schülern gelehrnt.*

But Mr. Nock has revealed himself of the
unhappy class of men whose state is more
pitiable a one. He belongs with those who do
not know, and utterly ignore it. It is this
that leads him to make the attempt to patron-
ize a lot of young people; a neither novel nor
unwonted occurrence; for the maxim which
declares "those who cannot do, set themselves
up to teach" is an old one. It is this self-
righteousness which deprives us of the help
he as well as every human being is in position
to give us and himself. And, it seems, we shall
have to prepare ourselves to do a long while
without the assistance of Mr. Nock. This is
by no means the first instance in which, under
the mask of friendliness he has demonstrated
his complete lack of sympathy for the strug-
glers. And it is distinctly the most aggressive.

The signs warn us, therefore, that in the class of those interested exclusively in their own figures, he is destined a long while to remain.

SIXTUS BECKMESSER

SIXTUS BECKMESSER

MEISTER SIXTUS BECKMESSER, town-clerk of the free imperial city of Nüremberg at the time of the *affaire* Walther von Stolzing, is usually represented a malevolent buffoon. Henlike of head-movement and hoarse of throat, a pasty pedant absurdly beribboned staggers round the stage most cruelly exposing himself to the jeers of the population, and not proof nor prayer can convince the world the figure is exaggerated. Alas the cosmic complexes! one might suppose it fated that the critic thrown by insensibility athwart the path of a novel beauty created in his own time should stand before posterity merely an ugly clown, so uncharitably have the failings of this one example been dealt with. Men will never believe that such misguided judges presented other than ridiculous aspects to the eyes of their townspeople, that Meister Sixtus, for example, was a most respectable character, considered throughout the city of Nüremberg and in Fürth as well an authority on the art of poesy. To not one of our singers and operatic producers has there ever come the impulse to correct their cruel picture of this historical personage by comparing it with some Beckmesser of our own time. Heaven knows there are enough of them about to give all a correct conception of the appearance of the learned Stadtschreiber. There's Mr. Royal Cortissoz, handsomely able to help us arrive at some conception closer to the original. There's Mr. Walter Pach, too, an excellent, oh an excellent model. Best of all, presenting the type with a truly classic purity, there is the superbly up and coming young Mr. Thomas Jewell Craven; a single look in his direction, and no longer could Beckmesser be played in gaudy ribbons. But all these magnificent opportunities are left to knock in vain. The world is not easily to be deprived of its favorite delusions; for many years to come persons who seek to reject by use of antiquated and scholastic criteria a fresh lyric loveliness will have to look forward to the unenviable fate of being remembered, if remembered they are at all, with contempt; their slight obtuseness regarded as poisonous; themselves in all their pathetic well-meaningness regarded merely as objects of coarse ridicule.

Unfortunate wretches, as though their blindness were not its own reward! For what else was the historical Beckmesser, for example, but the tragic person ignorant of the esthetic experience? Poor Sixtus, like his successors down to the Jewell of our own diadem, had merely never known what being in harmony with another object, springtide or photograph, sunset or painting by Michael Angelo, was. If he objected so strenuously to admitting to trial a poet who confessed himself inspired largely by an enthusiasm for nature, love, and profane song, it was merely for the reason that he himself had never experienced the "impulse from a vernal wood," and consequently suspected of prevarication those who pretended having had it. He seems to have trusted nothing save rules, formulas and intellectualizations. His suitability as lover he wished adjudged entirely on the ground of his esthetical qualifications, particularly his familiarity with the writings of Aristotle, Crocestotle and Roger Fryistotle. If he rejected Walther's hymn it was not entirely for the reason that he himself was a fearful and jealous competitor. He merely remained insensitive to the music, listening primarily for homage to his own con-

ception of "knowledge, reflection and a genius
for construction"; and, missing it, deemed he
had not been given "the emotional force of a
direct experience." Early in his career he had
fallen into the unfortunate habit of dogmatiz-
ing on matters into which he had not looked.
About him, there was always the background of
a philistine uncultured home, a "hard" adolescence, and the unfortunate experience of
apprenticeship to Magister Thomas Bramarbass. For Beckmesser, as the Beckmessers of
the world will always do, most unfortunately in
youth betook himself to the feet not of a master
who worked from feeling, but to those of an
intellectualizer of his own sort, a certain Bramarbass, famous in his time for a willingness
to assure the world that he knew all the secrets
of the art of poesy, and author of a number of
lifeless epics founded on analyses of Lucan and
Statius. Here, in the closet of this gigantic intellect, Beckmesser got corroboration and faith
and an avocation; here, with the aid of certain
crabbed treatises he acquired the esthetic jar-
gon which gave to his pronouncements the air
of authority and learning ever so impressive to
the general public. True, the poets, the lovers
of poetry, and the philosophers, were not al-

ways so greatly imposed upon. When Erasmus, Reuchlin and Hutten wrote to each other about the critiques of Meister Sixtus, which was not often, they used very much the selfsame tone employed by an authority on art now living in Florence in expressing himself about those of Mr. Craven: "He never has a word to say that is not the rattling of the tedious shibboleths of the last generation. He suffers severely from a colic of technical vocabulary. I would not know as much as he does, not if I were paid double. At least, I'd look it up in the encyclopedia before I said it." To the misfortune of all, however, neither Beckmesser nor the public of Nüremberg ever had the advantage of such valuable judgments. Had they, Beckmesser might have been saved from making his famous mistake about Walther's music and covering himself eternally with blame.

Besides, in those years, Nüremberg, although rapidly waxing in culture, prestige and power was still a little the provinces, its intellectual atmosphere a sort of alcohol preservative of mentalities which had become long since obsolescent in centers of art. Consequently, unquestioned of his townspeople, Beckmesser

continued to arbitrate in matters of poesy. No
work was considered classical in construction
did not he declare it so. No poet was held
modern before Sixtus had measured his verses
according to the precepts of Magister Bramarbass, and declared them continent of "the emotional force of a direct experience." He
imparted the solemnity of science to all poetic
criticism. With shudders he deplored the
broad emotional outbursts of Sachs. The
"amateur esthetician" was denounced; defended was the "common sense method."
So, every inch a dignity; fastidiously arrayed
in sable clothing edged with fur; decorous of
manner and precise of speech, Meister Sixtus
Beckmesser passed through the streets of
Nüremberg and entered places of assemblage
to the respectful salutations of the bourgeoisie.

And when finally he came to grief, the event
was not accompanied with the gay scandal we
have learned to associate with it. Beckmesser's serenade was not yodelled before
Pogner's house to the laughter of all Nüremberg. Rather, it was like the appearance of
Craven's novel *Paint;* noticed of only a few
spectators astounded that one who flaunted
austere critical standards should himself pro-

duce anything so flat, common and unfelt. Neither was the well-deserved drubbing at the hands of Buermeyer,—I mean at the hands of David the apprentice sorcerer—generally observed. We are used to seeing David thrash Beckmesser at the very front of the stage under the eyes of all the world. Yet here again *der alte Wahn* is active; such neat little jobs are never seen by the multitude. They inevitably take place before only a few interested persons. The world has always something better to do than watch collisions between town-clerks and angry apprentices, and sciolists and humanists, and remains ignorant of the fact that the floor is being wiped with human material.

Nor is it true that Beckmesser appeared in the lists of song during the tournament attired in the costume of a court-jester. He appeared as ever richly and soberly apparelled, and conducted himself with his usual great dignity. His language was precise and his delivery superb. But about that time not only the masters but the public as well began becoming aware of the emptiness of this martyr to intellectualism. And still it moves, even in Franconia; and in the light of a great day Beckmesser's tune was recognized obsolete; his singing, croaking: while the celebrated methods of Crocestotle and Bramarbass aroused laughter. They could not appear otherwise when placed beside the work of a man who had a living impulse to communicate; and as he stalked away poor Beckmesser was followed by the sound of the joyous plaudits greeting the singer whose song he had not heard. Hence, all who crowded about the judges' stand became convinced that the grave Herr Stadtschreiber had indeed that day appeared before them in ribbons, cap and bells.

It was only a wicked trick of Memory, fond of transposing into an outward and visible sign, a grace entirely spiritual and entirely inward.

BY WAY OF EPILOGUE: THE HOSPITAL

BY WAY OF EPILOGUE:
THE HOSPITAL

KNIFESHARP, a dull glitter, the hospital waits for us. They are for us, the pinching vise of pain, the hypocritical sweet of ether. They are for us the naked windows and the whitewashed steel. There is no sense forgetting the wicked edge turned usward, the iodoform and the ghastly bareness. The hospital is always there but a few doors removed from any house we may inhabit. It is always there, lurking behind the piles of the town that screen it. Off the sidewalk it opens wide its maw; from the careless traffic of the sidestreet it raises its drab walls and sleepless windows. Always that mouth takes in, always the rooms behind the empty panes are full of aching bodies. It may be a week, it may be a month, it may be a year, that it will wait, motionless. It may wait motionless for us two years, three. But each of us bears always in him a sickness twin to his wellbeing. Each of us bears within him a death

359

that is twin to his life. Sacs form themselves
in organs. We are born jangling discordant
orchestras of nerves; we steady ourselves, con-
trol them, and ulcers grow rank in the linings
of the canals. We do not welcome with open
arms the arrows of life; and the body hears our
secret prayer, and sickens, and commences suddenly to die. The organism cannot longer de-
fend itself unaided. Surgeons and anestheti-
cians are given mandates, created functions of
the helpless, manic frame. The fine steel edge
of the hospital, that has been waiting so stilly
but a few yards away, springs close, and bears
its knife upon us. It is we, at last, must go
pass through the maw. It is we must go be the
creatures who suffer the operating table and
the fumes of ether and carbolic acid. It is we
who are forced to come to know in our turn, the
lying prostrate, pain-ravaged, in the high iron
cot; the lying bare to the naked walls and windows, plaster and iodoform of agony; the lying
helpless beneath the indifferent lethargic tread
of hours that will not speed. We must go learn
the thrust of pain in the soft entrails; learn
what it is to be the feebly prostrate thing to
whom folk bring flowers, and who grows gray

with utter weakness after but few minutes' talk, and whom a woman has to lift.

The telephone-bell rang harmlessly in the dwelling-room, but through the receiver there jetted livid into the shelter the words seven feet high OPERATION TO-MORROW EIGHT A. M. REPORT THIS EVENING. The hospital has touched. Up to the ominous and electric moment in which the business-like pleasantness of the young lady secretary of the surgeon spoke, only the head had known the hospital. Even after physicians had declared a section imperative, only the head had known it. The quick had remained innocent of it. Now the quick, too, knows. The cold metal hand has laid itself on the center, and all about, pandemonium shrieks. About the suddenly paralyzed spot, an insane dissonant orchestra howls and gesticulates and clatters. Drums throb, strings shriek, horns gasp and roar while the words of doom rear themselves white and enormous. Impulses commence motions of flight. Impulses get up and try to push. A thousand voices babel evasion, defiance of doctors. Impulses get up and throw a few clothes hastily into a satchel and take the next train for Chicago from whence they telegraph to the

surgeon that the operation is indefinitely post-
poned. For pain is upon us, and we are found
naked defenseless against the imminent pain.
Naked, with the defenseless body, we are called
to meet the scaly monster. We have only the
white tender flesh to oppose to his claws, the
white sensitive flesh that every pin can wound.
And where should one get the science to meet
the onslaughts of pain? Where the technique
of passing the hours of embrace of the unknown might? They teach us politeness.
They train us how to serve ourselves with knife
and fork. Oh, yes, they train us not to drop
morsels of food from the lips, to clean our
mouths on napkins. But the science with
which to meet with the soft cringing flesh the
blows of pain, that they do not give us. We
can search frenetically all day long in our
memories for some gesture to make, some
method with which to meet and disarm the
dragon. There is none there. If the elders
knew it, they did not pass it on. Pain is coming; and we cannot find a spell to conjure it
away.

The dislocated orchestra wearies itself out.
The impulses start feverishly awhile, then tug
with lesser and lesser main. Something in one

must be careless whether the immense unknown threatens the innocent flesh. Something must be willing to combat the scaly beast naked and unarmed. Perhaps it is a greater fear that drives one; fear of the penalty of refusing the hospital's aid. Whatever it is, nevertheless in the self, where the telephoned words dug deepest, there solidifies a steel. The rest of the body, the fiddling and lamenting musicians, are compelled to obey. The steel makes preparations for the hospital calmly, as though ignorant of the fact that distress awaits it. The future patient finds himself, he does not know precisely in what manner it came about, coated, descending the stairs to where the taxicab waits, the affairs he has left behind him arranged. The flesh may cling supinely to the city objects it is compelled to give over. Serenades of misery may chant sweetly and mournfully in the blood. Magnificent farewells to the drivers of the trucks skirted by the taxi, to women mounting to the elevated railway tracks carrying bundles, may compose themselves all along the route. The chauffeur clutches the wheel and drives forward the car; the pillars of the elevated railway fall behind relentlessly one by one. The patient finds himself standing in the garishly lighted hospital office, giving the name and address of the next of kin who is to be notified in the eventuality that an "accident" transpire. Swiftly, the high nude room, in which he is to lie during the weeks after the operation, is entered and known. Clothing, cits' clothing, the right of those who walk the streets of the world whole, is abandoned in the tiny closet closed by the white-painted door. The hard high bed is mounted. The orderly with his razors and scissors and bottles comes for the business of depilating.

There must be many for whom the sojourn in the lazaret never becomes other than this, who pass through the great funnel of the place like captives of war dragged by soldiers in the train of a triumphator, and know only the cruelty of it. There must be millions who, even after the cot has been mounted and the pubis shaven, even after the section has been made and the ether-trance quit and the convalescence commenced, refuse to find within themselves the will to take the hospital to them and make the event their own, and draw from the happening an experience. One need not, after all, balance oneself upon the tight-rope of life. One is at liberty to elect to be shoved across it shrieking. The blows of the hospital can be received on the back. The misery can be rejected with wailing and complaint. Eight dollars the day hires a nurse who hearkens soberly to every whimper one may choose to emit. Drugs deaden the ache. Morphine unhooks legs and arms from one's trunk as though they were legs and arms of a porcelain doll joined by wire, lays them gently aside in the bed. The chamber where lie stored the weapons of the spirit can remain unopened. Only, to refuse the hospital the consent is to be doubly smitten by it; to leave it standing erect and dully glittering all the duration of life. Scarcely have the blander days of bed-riddenness come, than the old fear is on the patient once again. The edge is bared again, and threatens. Suddenly, over and over again, he remembers that, in but a few years time the knife will spring upon him once more, and submit him to fresh agonies. The hospital, he knows, is full of a thousand forms of pain that wait for their occupants as the cots in the wards wait for theirs. And into any one of them he may be fitted capriciously by the world machine, and compelled to make silly and meaningless gestures of suffering that have been rehearsed before myriad times to no end, and forced at last to die an anonymous death that is shabby from constant mean usage. Never does the hospital cease casting toward him its long shadow.

But another hospital, not edge and adamantine plane, can rise and wipe away the inhuman force and blind machine, and flourish in its stead. If millions of those who pass through the place feel only the brutal buffet, come forth smitten with their own ugliness and impotence and insufficiency, equal millions come to know an institution that is like a tall gaunt woman, not at all comely, not at all smiling, but nevertheless of a gracious touch, a thousand grave and tender ways, a white and healing presence. The lovers of life come to know this. To them, it shows its silver kindly visage. It does not crush, does not take strength away. When this gives back the body, it gives back a body purged of fear. Like a loved and loving woman, it can prove a bath of life. The hospital can show its sorcery on the very night when the lover for the first time lies in the stripped room and waits alone for dawn and the hour of the surgery. He, too, may have entered a herd of captives scourged to their goal by a single steel master. He, too, may have lain himself down unreconciled to the truth that to live is to give pain and receive it. But, scarcely is the orderly with his tray departed, than an old trick plays itself. The back that has hitherto been turned to the present sinks. Slowly, tranquilly, serenely, the breast that has been held away from it heaves upward, turns fully on the situation, and meets it warm. The frenzy of escape goes. The sense of utter destitution beneath an empty illimitable dome disappears. Misery of loneliness becomes joy of loneliness. Feeling of destitution becomes feeling of delight at being left alone to confront life unaided. Immense, the joy of being possessed of self, of being within his own proper skin, of being alive and there at that very moment, in that very place, rises through him, and floods his veins. Since he is here, the here may as well come on, whether it be pleasure or be pain. Even if it is hurtful, it is no less welcome. The patient, who an hour since was eager to flee his fate, hugs himself for the sense of power and ability that well in him, shakes his own hand as one shakes the hand of a good friend seen after a long separation. The world is here in this narrow room as

outside under the black vault of the sky. Even
were to-morrow to prove the last day, and the
ether-cloud never to part, and the street again
never to take up the lover, this night at least
feels the blood in him still jetting hot and
quick, the wonder of white linen and velvet
night-clouds still about him. The hospital, the
knife sharpness and the hurtfulness, have been
accepted.

Thick doors to muffle moaning were there, in
the room, a while since. There was a wash-
stand, from which nurses had carried water
and cloths to wash those too weak to serve
themselves. There was hung, pointing downward, up in the ceiling, an iron fixture, like the
the breast of a gigantic negress, within which
was hidden an electric globe ready to filter a
sickly light through sleepless night hours. Up
on the highest story of the hospital there was a
room where abdomens were slit daily and tubes
inserted. But they have disappeared, in that
hour of reconciliation. The whole outside has
been crowded back into shadow. It is the space
within the self that has become wide, stretched,
exclusive of the objects that were once so close,
pushing them back to find space in the universe
for themselves as best they can. If light there

is in the tiny apartment, it proceeds from within. The great space that fills the world is
suffused with secret shine. It is as though
in a tiny dark cabin a door had suddenly been
thrust open, and the light of myriad candles
reflected by lusters and mirrors been poured
into the somber place. For, in truth, a door in
the brain, long shut, has suddenly given, and
flooded forth a radiance that is not often seen,
and discovered a winged figure. The other
self, the self whose visitations are so rare, the
self with immense white pinions, is here, bend-
ing over the lover again. Her hand is upon his
skin. She is ever with him, she murmurs. She
will not let him go, she breathes. She holds him
tight in her embrace, sinks him into sleep.
And when morning comes she is not gone. She
is there when enters the nurse with the
morphine-loaded needle. She it is who assists
him into the humble apron-like hospital shirt,
the shirt that is ridiculously like a child's
frock, the shirt that patients must wear onto
the operating table so that they can be stripped
with a single jerk. Tittering and hilarious, she
mounts with him the gocart on which he is
wheeled to the operating room. She urges him
to laugh to scorn the sudden blinding blaze with

which the operating room bursts over him upon his carriage, faces with him the complex of bare glittering steel and murderous disinfectants and clusters of many fierce electric bulbs above the operating table; makes light of terrifying appurtenances, scintillation of the edges and surfaces of myriad objects of metal and glass, slaughter-house aprons of a crowd of attendants, enervating bustle and objectivity of the nurses and doctors, biting glare of the sun through glass roof into the hot place. They tie him to the table; tie him hand and foot, pull back the blanket from his body. But she breathes for him deeply, joyously, scornfully, into the ethercone; gulps with madness and defiance the warm sickish gas, forces it downward into the lungs and at last spreads over the head of the sick man the mantle of unconsciousness.

A galloping of black nightmare steeds. They shoot out, away, travel ten miles in an instant like the spinning lead horses 'bout a roulette wheel, disappear, and then are back, shooting out like bullets once again. . . . In the midst of a steel maelstrom that whirls and whirls and sucks there erects itself a pyramid of polished livid metal. It is small, but terrible and frigid

and threatening, and on it there is a number,
2 billion billion billions, and the pyramid is the
number and one cannot grasp it, it is too immense and the thing is sucking you in. . . .
Somewhere, in an illimitable floating space of
pure, untrammeled being color of nasty sweet
yellow, somewhere they are holding it under,
forcing it down, down, crowding it under with
a thumb. First, they are forcing it down in
the corner of the room, up under the ceiling.
Then, they are pushing fiercely on the upper
lip, and the voices all are near, and they say
"Diabetes and Bright's Disease," or "Cancer"
or "Tuberculosis of the Intestines." There is
a great crowd standing about the patient, he is
still in the operating room, he supposes. But
pain, searing pain, pain that beats in the
wound, is in his bowels. Someone, it appears
has struck him a ferocious blow, kicked him in
the abdomen, and over the stifling hot cloths
and blankets in the conservatory heat, the black
shades of the secluded sick-room define themselves. The operation is over; the table has
become a bed. Pain beats in the wound, returns with strength increased after each assault to beat again, to beat persistently in the
very quick of the wound. The crowd has

thinned to two nurses. The floor-nurse goes;
the other, the day-nurse, refuses water to the
ether-sick parching throat. But though pain
subtly parts leaf from leaf, subtly fingers its
way through the petals so that it can stab into
the very bud of the wound, the other self, the
self with wings, is still with the lover. What
health, what pleasure, could not achieve, the
domination of pain, the over-topping of fear;
that, in the space of a dozen hours of contact,
the hospital has already succeeded in teaching
him. Here, in the very furnace of the enemy,
amid his searing, broiling flames, a serene gesture sweeps over the fiery space. Since pain
clamors like a dog for the flesh, the flesh is
thrown before pain. Pain is permitted to lord
it as he will, to stab into the raw unintermit-
tently if he will. The flesh is thrown before
him so that he may glut himself to his content.
No defense against his hammering is made.
He has the body entire in his grasp. The hands
are lain passive on the breast. Passive before
his assaults the spirit itself lies. For the spirit
knows it cannot be attained, cannot be violated.
The spirit, pain cannot overwhelm, savagely as
he may attempt the storm. His renewed and
ever again renewed charges cannot lay low

the walls. They rise imperial above his grasp.
If time will not on; if it is only twelve o'clock
when it should be five, and only nine o'clock
when it should be one in the morning; if time
lags outside in the street like a drunkard, making no headway even when he seems to be on
his way, reeling impotently from wall to wall,
losing ground rather more than gaining it, he is
not spurred on, chided forward. Time may
fall in a heap in the gutter and lie prone, if
he will. Even should it appear that he will
nevermore stir again and resume his regular
march, he is left to lag as he chooses. For, high
above the fury of norseman Pain, the bulwark
stands. the towers rise, the crown floats high
and untarnished and inviolate.

Strange, the health, sometimes so fine, sometimes so coarse, the hospital makes to thrill
through its guest. Shortly after it has discovered to the patient the power of pride, it brings
close to the bedside a self which most folk do
not at all like to perceive, and fight and push
away whenever it threatens to creep out from
under their souls' clothing. This is a small
pudgy imp, a happy dirty little wretch, a
shameless infant Rabelais. Yet, for all his dis-
reputability, a triumph attends his release. The

excretory muscles, for a while before he shows
himself, refuse to labor. The unaccustomed
position of the patient in bed, the violence done
the nervous system, the anesthetics, have lamed
them. The cramp will not relax. Orders dis-
patched from the brain have remained un-
obeyed. The regent in the head has been de-
throned. His sovereignty is impaired. He
cannot find the gesture of command wherewith
to make his insurgent subjects resume their
allegiance. He is like an irate businessman at
the telephone, who, on uttering a number into
the transmitter, hears only the voice of the
operator say apathetically "Number please";
and on shouting loudly and yet more loudly in
the effort to make himself understood, hears always the same dull query "Number please" in
response. Internes with new instruments of
torture have to be summoned. Nurses with
tubes and hateful pans appear. Detestable
ceremonies have to be consented in. Humiliating presences have to be borne. Discomfiture
is complete; rage only makes it greater. Then,
of a sudden, an impish grinning snout gazes
inquiringly around the corner of the mind.
The sufferer had forgotten it a long, long while,
many, many years ago, forgotten entirely that

its owner existed. But he is here again. He takes charge. There is nothing the pudgy porker prefers to this sort of functioning. And he can do miracles. He makes superfluous and ridiculous internes and catheters and tubes and ceremonies. He installs himself under the covers, hops about and sings all day. He rings the bell that depends from the head of the bed over the pillows. He keeps the nurses running to and fro; winks at their crossness. The patient marvels that anyone can feel a like keen triumph in performing such quotidian acts. The puck crows with pride and with delight at his performances. His vaunting can scarce be suppressed. Whenever a visitor enters, he tries mightily to shout, "Just think I, I myself, completely unaided, have just succeeded in voiding."

And when pain has finally rested from his attacks, and given up the storm, and gone to find some other, weaker brother to besiege, and the single pillow underneath the neck becomes two, and finally three, the hospital breaks down another dam, and lets rush free in the sun another human and very different power. There was a world the lover knew well in the days when the sap had begun slowly to mount in

him. It was a world bewitching and hurtful,
full of magical things on which he might not
lay hand. Life, vaguely surmised, was rich
with an old mystery. Harp strings swept
faintly in all things, vibrated behind certain
hilltops caressed by the hand of afternoon, outside sundown windows, under star-powdered
firmaments. And so again a virginal wonder
transpires from his breast, and comes back to
him in the hues and hours of the earth outside
his sickroom panes. For now once more, he
is a slow, lingering gathering of sap, a long
vigil for the advent of the power that will permit him to move into his own course. The
days begin to stream in the direction of the
hour of discharge. The morning ceremonies
of bathing, and alcohol rubs commence to follow harder on each other. The world comes
tantalizing nearer with the visits of the callers
that can be endured a little longer each day.
All about, in this air of anticipation, there circulates the life of the young nurses, buzzes a
girlish, boarding-school excitement over plans
for graduation ceremonies, campaigns for
funds for the new nurses' home, confessions of
lovers and engagements, room-mate's secrets.
So when evening sunlight falls on the street

without the hospital windows, and creeps corn-colored along brick walls, the patient is once more the youngling whom mountain blue could make quiver and swim. Over the line of tenement roofs, the sky is the pale sweet wash of spring. Despite wintry weather and city roar, a green of budding trees makes itself to be felt, a shimmer of nascent foliage about black water-logged trunks announces itself. Evening clouds are Wagnerian purple in the sky. The horses of the Valkyrie charge through the twilight blue. Cloud apotheoses move away, smiling and beckoning with still, godlike gestures; move away adown the heavens. The cosmos is again a mysterious promise.

What final strength the hospital has infused, that is left to the last days of the sojourn to reveal. The outer world which begins to float in upon the patient whilst the usage of his limbs is being regained, and shoves toward him its fingers and capes and promontories as he wavers feebly from bed to chair and back again to the safe bed, is seen then to be no longer the one he quit, some weeks before. Indeed, the sunny tin roof onto which nearly every one is lifted during the last days of his recuperation, can prove a high place before which the

pageant of the laboring city unrolls in new
order. Some hand has touched, for the vision
of the convalescent, the belching factory chimneys, the cubes of sullenly bricked-in space, the
discolored leagues that lie across the parapet,
vasty beneath the smoke-hazed barrel-vault of
heaven; and turned away their edge; transformed their tendency. Before, there had been
a sprawling disordered pellmell that weighed
inexplicably upon the heart of him, a hoarse
chorus that swelled and roared from the four
corners of the windy sky. Like adults who hu-
miliate with their complete indifference the
child, there had risen above him the high
shoulders of office-buildings and warehouses,
escarpments of brick, fuming nozzles of fun-
nels, cumbrous ignoble bridges across which
crawled hour after hour an interminable pro-
cession of high-packed motor-trucks, an array
of mechanical ants dragging each its burden.
They would not off his chest. But now, they
are light upon it. River of cast metal, prison-
fortresses in the back yards of proud, grim
boroughs, sorcerer's kitchen, they have all become transparent, shrunk before forms greater
than they are.

For, during the days spent in the sick-room

below, death has been known. Sighted by the
patient has been the strange brother whom he
bears within him, and who will one day glut
himself upon him as life before has glutted itself. He had sighted it in others; seen the un-
ending tide of men and women and children
coming in living, going out living or dead, making way for fresh occupants who arrive, are
wheeled to the operating room, and descended
blue and unconscious, wrapped in antiseptic
cloths. He had perceived the silence and the
loneliness in which each is condemned to play
the supreme acts of his drama. He had felt the
immutable secretiveness of all existence. And
here, by his side on the roof overlooking the
city, there are young girls with drains in their
opened sides, children worn to sallow flaccid
bags by incurable maladies; many diseases of
the wretched body, many pitiful bundles of
sick humanity, many weary, yellow regards.

Death has been known in the flesh and accepted. And only through the touching and
realization of death does the loveliness of life
find way to us. For death stands always
and bids man gaze him straight in the eye,
and know the white by facing square the
black that lies upon it close, and gives

it value and gets value from it in its
turn. And the poets come, the modern
poets, offering their sense of tragedy that men
can be free to feel the reality of death and have a
joy in living. But men, unable to accept the
challenge, for only love can accept the fact of
mortality, try to blot out the visage of death,
try to build walls between them and it, to dis-
tract their own attentions by creating tasks
and goals that will enable them to forget the
nature of their careers on this planet. Here
then, between the riverways of a city, unwilling to make a single turning, a single orientation, and behold standing in the very midst
of their fictitious city the hospital and the
tomb, men sit burying their heads in an earth-
filling, heaven-scraping immensity of muck;
and lose with the black the white.

Once deciphered from the high platform to
which hospitals or poets lift the man, its reality has already commenced to pass. A field
there was, full at night of spooks and gib-
bering ghosts. But at the hour when a taxi
leaves a hospital port carrying a passenger who
has lived the lazaret through, the sun, rising,
shows the haunted place merely a verdurous
meadow, with gate-bars deposited upon the
ground.